Matthew Small is a fiction writer and freelance journalist, currently living and writing in the limestone city of Bath in south west England.

Matthew has travelled through many parts of the world exploring different cultures and societies across five continents. In 2012 Matthew embarked on a·trip to the Holy Land to further his political understanding of the area, which is documented in his debut book *The Wall Between Us*.

Visit Matthew at
thewordsisaw.co.uk
or on Twitter
@TheWordsISaw

Preface

Everybody has a story to tell. This is what I learned while attempting to further my understanding of the ongoing Israel and Palestine conflict. Unfortunately, these stories predominantly reverberate around suffering, hatred and lasting injustice. In short, they are painful to hear. And after having left these fertile and volatile lands, after hearing these tales and seeing humanity being lost to fear and distrust, what hope can one retain that peace will ever be mastered between these two deeply scarred neighbours?

Over the course of these reflections, I will do my best to capture my experience of a month spent in Israel and Palestine. It will recall my time spent in Jerusalem; of joining a group of Europeans and Israelis as we travelled into the West Bank to harvest olives with Palestinian farmers, incorporating meditation into non-violent activism; it will retell a meeting with a settler who lives in the controversial settlement of Shilo; and recapture encounters with different organisations which are determinedly trying to plough both lands for a sustainable future, whilst drawing on my own diary entries and my search for answers as to why this wall between us exists.

I am not an expert in this conflict; I am a writer who tries to find reason through writing.

In truth, and after two weeks spent listening to stories, I had almost come to the decision that I couldn't comment about this conflict. The history is too complex, the wounds too deep, and the helplessness I unknowingly wrote my way into was constricting. Who am I, an outsider, to think that I can do anything to help this situation?

However, this was soon changed by one little boy: Isam. I had joined him and his family in his father's olive groves in the rich soils surrounding the Palestinian town of Deir Istiya. By midday, the hot sun was beginning to take its toll, and in a moment of respite I took to collecting fallen olives in a plastic bucket, seeking shelter in the shade of the trees. Isam left the group and came to help me. Together, we sifted through the dry, crumbling soil, retrieving the bruised, purple olives. He suddenly looked up and gave birth to a few words that have inspired all that is to follow: "You give me the life in Palestine," he said, faltering over his English. "Talk the world!" he added. I was taken aback, unable to respond to this boy who had already returned to searching for more olives. "Talk the world," he said again, now pinching the source of his family's livelihood between his fingers. I was speechless. There was nothing I could say, no hope I could offer him. And in the patter of olives falling into the bottom of the bucket, the moment soon passed, and the harvest continued.

I cannot talk to the world; I do not have a strong enough voice. But of the few who I can talk to, you few who have taken it upon yourselves to share in these words, my only wish is that you too talk about the pressing need for peace to be again brought to the forefront of both Israel's and Palestine's interests. Presently, there is no political will for peace in Israel, or a strong united will for peace in Palestine. In fact, I would say that there is no real want by politicians to entertain the idea of peace. But in the will of the majority of people I spoke to, both Israelis and Palestinians, there was a real lust for peace. I fear that both are being gravely let down by their political leadership.

I do not want to cast judgement about who is right and who is wrong, the situation goes beyond this. But at the same time, I will not suppress my feelings and reactions to the things I saw. Sitting here now, with the November chill whispering through my window and the winter sunshine light and playful outside my family home in the New Forest, the memories I hold onto from my trip to the Holy Land already seem distant. Did I really depart from the intoxicating and soothing spirit of Tel Aviv just yesterday? Still, today, I know that both sides suffer, Israeli children and Palestinian children suffer, and that is why I have titled this book,

The Wall Between Us. We are all children of this one Earth; even if we can't see the concrete or the barbed wire fences, we are still impacted by their existence – our humanity is one, after all.

My hope is to share with you that even in the midst of conflict, bridges can be formed and relationships encountered – the seeds of peace can still be nurtured.

The Holy City

In his hefty biography, *Jerusalem*, Simon Sebag Montefiore embarks on what appears to be an impossible mission, bringing the complex story of the Holy City to life. I stumbled over the scale of his endeavour as I passed under Damascus Gate, first entering into the Old City of East Jerusalem with darkness sheltering in the narrow stone streets and my backpack heavy with excitement. My month in the Holy Land had begun, and where better to begin than in the Holy City itself, where Heaven and Earth are said to meet.

I could feel its immense history seeping out of the ancient architecture. The dark alleyways housed a sombre silence with the shops all barred shut as the night continued to veil the slip of a starless sky above. I hurried on, looking back and forth in search of my hostel, passing a group of Arab men sitting on low plastic chairs sharing a *shisha* pipe, smoking silently together.

The complex, turbulent and often bloody past of Jerusalem called on Montefiore to write a book of no less than 600 pages. I will write only, while conscious of my brevity, that the Old City is home to the holiest sites of the three Abrahamic religions: the Temple Mount with the Western Wall for Jews, the Dome of the Rock and the al-Aqsa Mosque for Muslims, and the Church of the Holy Sepulchre for Christians.

Since the 6th century BC, Jews have hungered over the return to the "Promised Land", after their Diaspora began with the destruction of Solomon's First Temple on the Temple Mount, in 587 BC. After an armed Jewish uprising in 70 AD, the Romans destroyed the Second Temple that Herod had built over the foundations of Solomon's. Jews were no longer able to worship freely at the foot of the Temple Mount, where according to the Torah the "Divine Presence" eternally rests, until the end of the Six Day War in 1967.

The birth of the Zionist movement, with the ideology of Jews returning to their "historical and biblical" homeland, had not made much progress until the turn of the 20th century. The fall of the Ottoman Empire saw the land of Palestine under the rule of a British mandate, governing over the people and territory until "such time that they are able to stand alone". The mandate was presupposed by the Balfour Declaration of 1917, stating that: "His Majesty's government view with favour the establishment in Palestine of a national home for the Jewish people, and will use their best endeavours to facilitate the achievement of this object, it being clearly understood that nothing shall be done which may prejudice the civil and religious rights of existing non-Jewish communities in Palestine, or the rights and political status enjoyed by Jews in any other country."

What the British did not expect was the commitment and longing of the early Zionists to self-determination. The atrocities that befell European Jews during the Second World War, with many countries closing their borders to the fleeing and desperate Holocaust survivors, caused a steady mass migration of Jews to land on the shores of Palestine. After armed conflicts with the Arab population, and using force against the British, the Zionists triumphantly declared, on May 14th 1948, the existence of the independent State of Israel, with West Jerusalem as its capital.

However, this triumph was a tragedy for the Palestinians, with an estimated 700,000 fleeing or expelled from their homes after the day of *Nakba*, meaning catastrophe, which is still commemorated each year on May 15th. Today, many millions of these refugees and their descendants still live in exile, unable to return to the ancestral land of their childhood. The enduring Israel/Palestine conflict was born, with sixty years of bloodshed, violence and loss now suffered by both sides, without an end in sight.

In 1948, the State of Israel was set within the Green Line, named for the green ink used to draw the borders on the map, but the Six Day War also gave Israel control of what is today's West Bank from Jordan, and the Gaza Strip from Egypt. Israel commenced a militarised occupation of these lands. The war also saw the annexation of East Jerusalem, bringing the Old City and its holy sites under Israeli authority, allowing Jews to again return to their "Holy of Holies".

Stopping with my thoughts, I turned to look back at the three men inhaling the flavoured smoke deep into their lungs. Coming down the street behind me, two Israeli soldiers strolled slowly past the smokers, carrying big black guns before them and wearing big black boots on their feet. They appeared young and out of place in their green army uniforms amongst the quiet streets, but I was to learn that guns and holiness go together in Jerusalem.

It was the nature of the occupation that was to be the focus of my time in both Israel and Palestine – I wanted to know what occupation looks like, feels like, and whether or not it is justifiable. But above all, I wanted to know why it persists.

A new wind rushed past me as I continued on my way, lifting the rubbish that speckled the dark stone into the dry Middle-Eastern air. Church bells rang out, echoing off the silence. I soon arrived at the Via Dolorosa; the street made famous by Jesus' final steps, weighed down by the heavy cross of his crucifixion. I wondered if having Christ pass this way was going to make my bed in the dormitory more expensive. I stopped before two large deeply-knotted wooden doors, and the entrance to The Austrian Hospice. I pressed on the buzzer, already tasting the cool beer that I knew waited within. My journey to the Holy City was over, but Jerusalem by night was a songbird compared to the feverish devotion and crowded streets of the daylight hours to come. My real journey had not even begun.

The Holy City, Religion and a Viennese Coffee

The Austrian Hospice, situated in the heart of the Old City of Jerusalem, is a speck of tranquillity in a sandstorm of religious fever, crowded streets and the cries of Arab market-traders. Completed in 1858, the hospice opened as a pilgrim's house, accommodating the rising number of pilgrims seeking to pay homage to Jerusalem's holy sites. During the war years, it served as a hospital, and only returned to its original purpose in the 1980s. I had not considered myself to be a pilgrim, but in their exhibition, *In Search of the Lord God*, the hospice regards a pilgrimage as nourishing the soul "in all the insight and solace that we can gain". Now I liked the sound of that.

So the first day of my *pilgrimage* began by tiptoeing out of the basement dormitory, pursued by the ruptured snoring of a fellow guest – still going strong in the early morning. Rubbing the lack of sleep from my eyes, I cursed him inwardly as I stumbled into the bright light of a new day, with Jerusalem flaunting her stone beauty before me. I stood in the centre of the rooftop, alone and turning to capture it all: The Dome of the Rock on my left mirrored the rising sun in its golden roof; on my right, the bells of the Church of the

Holy Sepulchre were ringing melodically, and behind me a house rising above all others was adorned in four blue and white Israeli flags, drooping in the still air.

In the Old City of Jerusalem you will find Jews, Muslims and Christians all living and worshipping inside of the great stone wall that once acted as the city's defences. Looking far into the view before me, I wondered where the problem was – why can't people just live together in harmony? Actually, I was starting to chew over my first questions about the occupation. Is it motivated by religion, the quest for land, or enforced in the name of security? I would have to get off this rooftop. I could at least try to get my head around one of these potential causes: religion. I was in the Holy City after all. But before all else, I promptly skipped back down the stairs and straight towards the hospice's café, in anticipation and need of my first Viennese coffee.

7th October

Sitting on a very old stone step outside the Church of the Holy Sepulchre, the air is ridden with church bells and the scatter of conversations off the white-stone square, largely coming from the group of tourists before me. I've walked through the Old City for around an hour; each street I took to reach the

15

Temple Mount I was turned back by the IDF (Israel Defense Forces). I think it's a religious holiday and therefore restricted to tourists. I did make it to the observation point for the Western Wall. It's quite a sight — the large courtyard before it was filled by Jewish worshippers, and waves of devotions were breaking over the wall itself. Then you come to the Holy Sepulchre, which is not so energised. Tourists are allowed into the church while the different denominations give services, and it's a hive of camera flashes and prostrations over The Stone of Anointing, on which Jesus' body was said to have been prepared for burial. It's funny to be somewhere so close to where Christ is revered and regarded to be felt most. I feel him very little here, and don't see his teachings in the core of this church. It's all devotion and no action.

What Jerusalem is very good at, if not drawing up the question of God, is to make one feel very hungry. I had found little in the sense of occupation so far, and of course wouldn't have expected to either, apart from the armed soldiers seeming to appear at most street corners. So I closed my notebook, still watching the hordes of tourists and pilgrims entering and leaving the church, before standing up from my step and fighting my way back to the Via Dolorosa and Abu Shukri's hummus restaurant that, like the passing on of a great mythical story, had been highly recommended.

Refuelled by a large bowl of hummus, and weighed down slightly by two white pita breads and a handful of falafel, I was ready to step outside the Old City; how does West Jerusalem compare? Passing back through Damascus Gate by daylight, in a slow train of sweaty people, you immediately arrive at the East Jerusalem Bus Station, with destinations such as Bethlehem and Ramallah displayed on the stands. I walked by, watching the number 21 bus to Bethlehem depart, heading for the West Bank and, despite all the media portrayals, a still-mysterious place. Somewhat distracted, I mounted the new city tram and headed for the Holocaust museum, Yad Vashem.

A good piece of advice for anyone visiting Israel is to make a note of the dates of religious holidays. Unlike in England, with Christianity's insistence on Sunday being the "day of rest" taken with a pinch of salt in order for capitalism to dominate each and every day of the week, in Judaism and Islam, Friday is the Holy Day. So from a little before sundown on Friday and lasting until sundown on Saturday, practising Jews will not partake in any creative act, be it work, play, or simply driving. This is the *Sabbath*.

"What do you mean, *closed?*" I said to the man in the little glass booth at the entrance to Yad Vashem. "It's Sunday, the *Sabbath* ended last night," I protested, uncertain why everything seemed closed to me, like the Temple Mount I had also failed to see. "*Sukkot*," I was told bluntly before being directed away.

In my naivety I hadn't even realised that we were entering into one of the biggest festivals in the Jewish year, *Sukkot*, the remembrance of God protecting the Israelites in the desert. I soon discovered that this meant the tram back to Damascus Gate was also out of service, and my pace quickened as I headed towards the nearest bus stop, hoping they were still running. This was when I met a Jewish man from Illinois, waiting at the bus stop, who also gave me my first insight into Judaism.

He was a rotund man with an American accent and manner that made him seem more like a tourist than a practising Jew coming to share in the *Sukkot* celebrations with his family that lived in Jerusalem. Still, we boarded the bus and struck up conversation.

"You're from England?" he asked, as we began to speed down the hill towards the centre of the New City. "Yes," I said, watching the blur of Jerusalem passing by outside the window with the shops beginning to close despite it still being early afternoon. "And what do you do?" he added. "I study religion," I said, still finding it strange to admit to people that I'm an aspiring writer who seeks to find an understanding of life through stories. He then promptly told me that, "You could never understand Judaism, unless you are living it!"

This caused me some discomfort, because from my understanding you can't really 'live Judaism'. You are born Jewish, or in rare cases pass the difficult procedure of converting to Judaism. I looked back out of the window, pondering his point that it is a living religion, a faith that enters every sphere of an individual's existence. Something told me that these insights would be useful when I made it to the West Bank, and confronted by the religious Jewish settlements that I had read so much about.

"What's that man doing with the horn?" I asked, pointing outside as the bus slowed at a junction with an orthodox Jew sounding a horn down the pavement. "He's telling the shops that it's time to close," the man from Illinois replied. "He can do that?" I added, watching the orthodox Jew now shouting as some of the shops were slow to let down their shutters. "If they want to hold onto their *kosher* licences then they will have to shut."

The term *kosher* is used to refer to food that conforms to the *Kashut* (Jewish dietary law), but it also appears to be used for abiding by the Torah, like the shops shutting for the commencement of *Sukkot*. I said goodbye to my friend from Illinois as we disembarked at Jaffa Street, the main high street that runs through West Jerusalem. It's very cosmopolitan, with shops you'd find in London, Paris, Sydney or all around the world for that matter.

I was amazed how quiet the city had become, religion had brought it to a standstill. There were no trams passing by and only a stirring silence strengthened as the sun dipped behind the fresh concrete buildings. I ambled back to the Old City, with an American accent still whispering in my mind, *You could never understand Judaism, unless you are living it.*

Some hours later, and still full from my rich hummus lunch, I indulged in a Goldstar dark lager dinner, an Israeli beer that tasted distinctly holy after walking around in the balmy heat of Jerusalem for a day. I settled on the terrace outside the Austrian Hospice, overlooking the Via Dolorosa, with five IDF soldiers resting amongst the shadows in the street below. I watched them laughing and joking together, wondering if they had just come out of college to continue their education in the army, which is mandatory for all Israel's children. What did they think about having to stand there into the night, watching the orthodox Jews pass them by on their way to the Wall, celebrating *Sukkot*, or the table of Arab men watching them from the restaurant opposite the hospice, or being photographed by the tourists who perhaps had never seen so many guns before? What education were they getting? What was their purpose for being there – security?

I sipped at my beer, watching these seemingly teenage soldiers, with their weapons held so naturally in their hands. My day in Jerusalem was at its end, and tomorrow would lead me to the birth place of Christ and into an ongoing occupation. My pilgrimage was destined for Bethlehem, and all the insights that this would bring. I swallowed the last of my beer, thinking about the hospice's definition of a pilgrim: "In their search for truth and authenticity every individual is called upon to examine God's calling in their own life."

How do we begin to look for the truth? Is it hidden from us, or do we hide it from ourselves? I left my vantage point with the call to prayer now ringing out of the speakers on top of a nearby mosque. I headed down to the basement and my bed, my ears already alert for the slight ripple of a snore.

Christ's Concrete Manger

The road to Bethlehem was smooth, the black tarmac fresh and winding. Once I was outside the suburbs of Jerusalem the world began to unfold, and waves of rising and falling hilltops formed a wide expansive sea stretching far into the hazy horizon. I sat with my notebook on my lap as the bus suddenly passed through a large patrolled checkpoint with cars queuing on the opposite side of the road. We had travelled from one Holy Land to another. Leaving Israel I was instantly met by a large scar of concrete that put the road into shadow as we went alongside it. I was now in Palestine, and my mouth fell ajar at the sight, sheer scale, and tragedy of the Separation Wall.

The Israeli West Bank barrier is, once completed, to be roughly 700 kilometres of fence and thick concrete wall that will separate the West Bank from Israel. It is now the most visible physical icon of the occupation, with the Berlin wall appearing like a baby compared with the sections I continued to observe as the bus left the highway, now taking the Bethlehem exit. The wall's construction is highly controversial in Palestine, in the eyes of the international community and even in parts of Israeli society.

However, the majority of Israelis support

the need for the barrier, seeing it as the only solution in stopping the terrorist attacks that so plague this conflict, sadly diminishing any chance of peace with each occurrence and unfortunately seeing the Palestinians often regarded as being a "nation of suicide bombers". But contrary to the argument of security, many claim that the wall is a means of annexing more of the West Bank, giving Israel extra land outside of the Green Line, and thus taking it from Palestinians. I didn't have long to form my own opinions about the wall; it was already snaking away in the bus' rear window as we began descending the thin dusty roads into Bethlehem, and the esteemed biblical birthplace of Christ.

Disembarking the number 21 bus at the crossroads in central Bethlehem, you are instantly hit by the pulsating tempo of the city; cars sound their horns as they jostle past one another on the busy roads, and sweet scents of the street sellers successfully seduce you on the walk to Manger Square. It's a noisy and stimulating welcome. You then arrive in the square itself, lined by benches, the Peace Centre café and the Church of the Nativity opposite the Mosque of Omar. I lowered my backpack and watched the lines of pilgrims streaming out of the church; the taxi drivers hovering around them were calling out: "Dead Sea! Banksy Graffiti! Apartheid Wall!" On the roads, Palestinian policemen were

Manger Square, turning the paper map I had picked up from the tourist information upside down, poorly attempting to find my bearings.

Leaving the chaos of the city centre, I walked into a quiet residential street where three small children were sliding down a steep tarmac hill on what looked like old school textbooks. Their cries of joy rang out like the bells of a church. I smiled as they began waving at me while continuing to ski their books in great excitement, leaving bits of torn paper behind them like flakes of snow. I carried on, now passing two older boys challenging each other to jump up and touch a road sign.

"Hello, where are you from?" one of them called, successfully slapping the metal sign. "England," I said, stopping to shake their hands. Both the boys' faces lit up. "Ah, Manchester United! Rooney! Rooney!" they cheered. "You like?" I asked, with their response being given in the rapid nodding of their heads. I left the boys chanting the names of Spanish and English football teams, as I traced the hill downwards, with the dusky sky being painted rose and the large Israeli settlement of Har Homa (built on land annexed by Israel following the Six Day War), now spreading out across the distant view. "Where the hell is this hostel?" I uttered with the straps of my backpack digging into my shoulders.

My hostel was owned by a welcoming

and obliging Christian. It appeared more like a home than a hostel, and I alone was to make use of it. I didn't mind and as the final call to prayer echoed through my open window, I thought about the course of our existence, the little children I had seen playing in the streets and the prison-like wall that shrouded their homes and lives. I considered what the birthplace of Jesus now symbolised, and what this portrayed about humanity. Before embracing sleep, I wrote this poem:

Bethlehem
When I said to you,
Be free little brother.
Why did you not run
across the hills where the olives grow
green?
Why did you not sing
of all the joy that life can bring?
Why did you not laugh
with the laughter of a silent sunbeam?
Why, little brother, are you still here?
You must not have heard me,
I said be free.

The Lasting Camps

Sitting back on a stone step in Manger Square, the call to prayer has just finished and the sun is letting its late morning sunbeams fall on the pilgrims leaving the coaches for the Church of the Nativity. Two young Palestinians are sitting beside me, drinking coffee and talking. One is tapping his foot on the stone to the Arabic music coming from the souvenir shop behind us.

So after an undisrupted sleep, I came here to pick up some bread for breakfast and a coffee served by a lad in the centre of the square. He poured it from a golden coffee pot, and seemed to put hot coals in the top of it. I soon savoured the strong taste of cardamom. I'm beginning to fall in love with Arabic coffee! Following breakfast, I took a sherut (shared taxi) to Dheisheh camp. You pay like two or three shekels and they take you to where you need to go – a great way to get about.

The camp is really just a hillside of deprivation; it's ghostly to walk around, with no hustle and bustle like central Bethlehem. There was a small group of people buying fruit out of plastic boxes, and again they were extremely friendly.

Two boys stopped to say hello and one was very willing to pose for a photo; they were sixteen. On my way back out of the camp, I was amazed to see a small bakery operating from inside one of the tin-roofed houses. Small round pita breads were falling out of a big oven into a wooden tray. The young man operating it was happy for me to take a photo, and then he insisted on giving me one of the freshly baked breads. I tried to pay him but he wouldn't accept anything. It's amazing to think that he lives in one of the oldest and poorest refugee camps in the West Bank, and yet he still finds more value in giving rather than receiving.

I held onto that warm bread as I walked back out of Dheisheh camp, pondering over what had become of a *temporary* refugee camp, with tents initially providing shelter to 3,400 Palestinians following the Arab/Israeli war in 1948. Today the camp is a web of narrow streets lined by breeze block buildings, housing almost 13,000 registered refugees living in a sterile and oppressive air. A small boy, perhaps five years old, ran past me kicking the litter at his feet into the air and singing. I wanted to leave, the bread now cooling in my hands and my appetite diminished by the sickness swelling in my soul.

According to the United Nations Relief and Works Agency (UNRWA)[1], in Dheisheh "a third of people are unemployed, with job opportunities restricted by the inaccessibility of the Israeli labour market." UNRWA also states that "15 per cent of the shelters are not connected to the public sewage system, instead using latrines connected to percolation pits." I turned to watch the little boy fading into the heart of the camp. What future can he hope for, other than walking down these squalid streets?

The refugees are not confined to Bethlehem alone, despite there being three camps all within a five-minute drive from Manger Square. The UNRWA records there to be in all nineteen refugee camps in the West Bank, with 748,899 registered refugees. All the camps are faced with the same problems of unemployment, overcrowding, and inadequate infrastructure. This also neglects the psychological repercussions of living a life such as this, without space to roam, parks for children to play in, along with an existence perpetually overshadowed by lasting poverty.

Waiting on the edge of the busy road outside Dhisheh for a taxi to take me back to the centre of the city, I saw a metal turnstile that had once been used to control the entry and exit to the camp by the IDF, most likely in the name of *security*. I was starting to hear this word used often. The turnstile now stands as a lasting reminder that at one time the occupants of the camp had had a life outside of this, with big metal keys suspended from its rusty bars; the keys that once opened the doors to their homes.

"Hey you, you can come with us!" I turned back to the road to see a yellow *sherut* pulling up and a young Palestinian man waving at me, smartly dressed with gelled-back hair. I hurried over and got in, shaking hands with my new friend, Jamal. "Thanks for waiting," I said to him, passing my two shekels forward to the driver as Jamal scrutinised my accent. "You're English?" he said, with his own English being pretty perfect. I nodded while trying to find my seatbelt as the driver suddenly stamped his foot down on the accelerator, and we rocketed away from Dheisheh camp.

It turned out that Jamal was once a tour guide in the city, but was now studying Geography and the Environment at university. "Interesting," I said, listening to him talk about his studies. But he simply sat back in the seat beside me, shaking his head. "In other countries *interesting* – but not here," he said.

Being Palestinian means Jamal is restricted in the countries he can travel to. There are no airports in the West Bank, and in order to travel to or through Israel, Palestinians are required to apply for permits, which are notoriously difficult to obtain, especially for young men, helplessly fitting the age and profile of *potential suicide bombers*. Presently, Jamal, even with his future degree, has very little chance or hope of seeing the geography of lands outside his own. I attributed the pensive expression that came over him as a response to the realisation of this fact, but then he smiled and asked, "How are you enjoying your time in Palestine?" "It's going great!" I replied, as the taxi's horn screamed out at stationary cars ahead.

After parting from Jamal at the taxi stand, I made my way slowly back through the busy streets towards Manger Square, deviating to check out the vibrant fruit and vegetable markets that provided an unquestionable assertion of the fertility of the surrounding countryside. I was dazed by the abundance and freshness of the produce for sale. However, I soon stopped amongst the stalls and looked around, not seeing a single tourist in sight. Surely all the people I'd seen disembarking the coaches at the Church of the Nativity would also want to see some of the real treats that Bethlehem had to offer? Did they just come to pay homage to Christ, and then get back on the coach to be whisked off to Jerusalem to pay homage to him some more? I felt sorry for them, missing out on such a profound experience as the life found in this Arabic market.

Settling on a table outside the Peace Centre café in Manger Square, I quickly ordered a Taybeh (Palestinian brewed beer) and opened my notebook. I wanted to make a note of the presence of the international aid I'd already seen in Bethlehem; the medical centre in the Dheisheh camp and the waste-collection lorries donated by Japan, along with some of the streets off Manger Square being refurbished through funding from Norway and Italy. But I was pulled away from my writing by a group of young Germans who were being addressed by a Palestinian on the next table. I held my pen between my fingers, doing my best to hear what he had to say.

9th October

Sitting on a stone column outside the Church of the Nativity, a group of European Franciscan monks and a cluster of nuns are to my right, and a Palestinian tour guide on his mobile is to my left, while the sun is setting beyond the buildings lining Manger Square before me. I'm enjoying the last of its presence. I tried my best to listen to a conversation taking place at the Peace Centre cafe today. A freelance journalist (Palestinian) was talking to a group of aspiring German writers. I caught bits of what he was saying and of course it was focused around some of the sufferings faced by Palestinians. According to him, the big settlement of Har Homa, visible on a hilltop outside Bethlehem, used to be an old forest, which was removed and the hilltop flattened to build on.

Presently, unless there is a miracle of change in global consciousness, I don't see how the land that is left to the Palestinians will ever really be theirs. The sun appears to have set behind the mosque on Manger Square.

Sweet Sage Tea and an Unexpected Tour

Bethlehem's Peace Fountain was glistening in the morning light, sunbeams reflected off the water along with the silver foil of a chocolate bar wrapper, peacefully floating on its surface. I hovered around it, waiting. "My Friend! My Friend!" a booming voice came from above. I looked up to see a heavy figure quickly pacing down the hill, with a silver drinks tray swinging at his side from his day's first deliveries. This was the man I had been waiting for; he'd promised me that he made the finest coffee and sage tea in all the West Bank.

"Your shop was empty," I said, as we shook hands. "Come, come!" my new friend replied, hurrying ahead to a road leading away from the fountain, where he entered a small cavern of a place emitting Arabian aromas to die for. "Sit! Sit!" he commanded, placing a plastic stool and wooden chair cushioned by an old rug in the narrow pedestrian street outside. "You like coffee or tea?" he asked. I wanted to try his renowned sage tea, I really did, but I succumbed to my need, or maybe it was my dependence. "Coffee," I said, settling down on the chair. "Yes, yes, coffee first and tea later," he said delightedly, before disappearing inside and beginning to boil some water over a small gas cooker. "Where you go today, Dead Sea?" I sat for a moment, weighing up his question. "Hebron," I called back. "Ah, Hebron," his whisper drifted with the smell of boiling coffee outside. "Good markets," he added, before continuing to stir the bubbling black liquid silently.

My only insight into Hebron, the largest city in the West Bank and located just 30 km south of Jerusalem, had come from an award-winning comic book series, *Palestine*. Its creator, graphic journalist Joe Sacco, had spent two months in the West Bank and Gaza during the early 90s and the first intifada. He introduces Hebron with an image of three young Jewish settlers, wearing *kippahs* on their heads and holding Uzis in their hands as they march down a city street. Through words and detailed sketches, he relates how Hebron had been a mean place for Jews; stating that many Jews in Hebron were massacred in the 1929 Arab riots. However, this all changed after Israel took control of the West Bank following the Six Day War. Immediately, fundamentalists made it their firm aim to settle in the Holy City, first occupying parts of downtown Hebron in 1979, with no concern for the Arab residents that already lived there, or need for governmental approval to justify their actions. Sacco concluded that the settlers were here to stay, drawing them with guns in hand.

I quickly savoured my friend's rich and cardamom-heavy coffee, dressed his palm with a few shekels and said I'd be back for tea later. "Okay, you not be disappointed!" he yelled, already loading his silver tray for more deliveries. Suppressing the flutter of my heartbeat, I walked out of central Bethlehem, got into a parked *sherut* and was immediately on my way to Hebron. Unknown at the time, this was to be my first of two visits to the city, which was actually a good thing because there is a lot to get your head around, in order to try and understand what the hell is going on in this place. But first, we must again turn to history before we can try and make any sense of the present. Why is Hebron of holy significance?

It can mostly be put down to one man, Abraham. The best known of the biblical patriarchs, Abraham plays a significant role in all three monotheistic faiths. Regarded by both Christians and Jews as the father of the Israelites, he is also a prophet in Islam and seen to be an ancestor to Mohammed. So Abraham's coming to ancient Hebron, also referred to as the City of the Patriarchs, was inevitably going to lead to religious tensions and trouble further down humanity's path. Setting this in motion, Abraham chose to bury his cherished wife, Sarah, in a cave and was later buried there himself along with Isaac, Jacob, Rebecca and Leah, who are all considered to be patriarchs and matriarchs by both Jews and Muslims. This has become the venerated Tomb of the Patriarchs, located in the centre of the city.

So coming back with this information to today, we find ourselves in a city with its holiness second only to the Temple Mount in Jerusalem for Jews, and which is deemed one of the four holiest sites in Islam, where Mohammed is also said to have stopped on his night journey to Jerusalem. There is much more to say as to why this city is so special in the eyes and souls of the religious, but I've got to get on because my taxi has pulled up and my fellow passengers are all pushing past me as they try to get out.

The drive to Hebron had been another blur through the olive-filled lands of Palestine; the taxi driver barely braked as we passed by disused checkpoints and donkeys laden with sacks of olives on the sides of the roads. I've a feeling that in the recent past, a trip to Hebron might have taken much longer, but the Israeli checkpoints were now just horrible concrete monuments of a war that sometimes rages more, and sometimes less, in this intense region of perpetual conflict. However, now filtering into the busy streets of Hebron, I didn't sense much in the way of conflict and was soon walking with another stupid paper map that only served to get me lost completely.

"Hello, my friend, what are you looking for?" I had been strolling down a covered market, with Levi's jeans stacked in piles on the tables, and Nike trainers of all shapes and sizes scattered around them. The young man who had called at me approached; "Hello, my friend, what are you looking for?" he said again. "Oh, nothing really," I replied, "I just want to get a sense of the place." My new friend was around nineteen years old, wearing a shirt and a smile that I thought I could trust. "Can I give you a tour? I give tours. Can I give you a tour of my city? I will show you occupation." I didn't take long to think over his proposition. "Okay," I said.

So my unexpected tour of Hebron commenced. My friend began by leading me back down the covered market before stopping at a turning to another street that I had obliviously passed by, my head being lost in my map. This street was barred by a high steel fence. "Right," my friend announced, "do you find anything strange about this street?" I looked again, seeing the closed shops and rubble scattered on the ground. "It's deserted," I said. He nodded, telling me that since the second intifada, this street, along with many others in the centre of the city, had been closed to the Palestinian residents that had lived there, along with the city's inhabitants that had once brought their daily groceries from this since abandoned commercial hub. "The intifada ended in 2004, yet they still won't let us return to our homes. Why is that?" My friend's voice shrilled, "Why?"

I had no idea. So we continued; I obligingly followed his commands. "This way, this way," he kept saying, almost secretively. One thing I did know about Hebron was that it is divided by rule; the Palestinian Authority is in control of most of the city, known as H1, and Israel commands a smaller militarised section, H2. I had no idea though that this is where my friend wanted to take me.

Turning a corner, we began making our way towards a Portakabin that had been turned sideways to fully block off the street before us. "H2," my friend said, pulling me towards the door of the cabin with the bold word *Entrance* held over it. "I'm allowed in there?" I asked. "You're fine with me," my friend assured me as we passed through the metal detectors that filled the inside of the cabin.

On the other side, I was stopped by a rather surprised-to-see-me soldier, who began sifting through my bag before asking to see my passport. "I have friends in London," he said simply, flicking through the stamps I had collected. I told him that if he ever goes to see them then he should visit Bath, a city that has always captured my heart and pen. "Good to know," he replied, handing back my passport and returning to the shade provided by a small parasol, waving me on. "This way, this way," my friend implored. We walked away from the cabin, with a trickle of Palestinians flowing through the metal detectors behind us. These were people whose properties fell into H2 Hebron, and every day they have to pass this soldier and through this Portakabin in coming to and from their homes.

The street we were now heading down was empty; the green doors of the shops that lined it were welded shut. Israeli flags were hung above them, with yet more Israeli flags painted onto the buildings' stone fascias. Ahead was a 400-strong Jewish settlement, one which had grown out of a few ambitious squatters in 1979. It was hard to keep bringing to mind that this was the centre of a city that has around 200,000 Palestinians living in it. This street was fit for ghosts and stirred an uncomfortable feeling that something nasty had taken place here.

"No! Not that way, I'll be shot if we go that way," my friend said, instead leading me up a hillside that would take us to a hidden Palestinian village. He began to talk about some of the aggressive acts that the settlers had used in forcing the Palestinians out of their homes, and said that even today the stall holders on the street beyond this one, in H1, are plagued by a barrage of eggs and stones that come from the rooftops commanded by the settlers. "They want us to leave the city entirely," he sighed.

On the hilltop, we stopped and looked out over the empty street and the new white stone building that was the settlement's synagogue. Stationed around this settlement there are said to be 4,000 soldiers, and their presence was felt, seen and unhindered. My friend led me on, passing his "Holy Land" with olive trees popping with green olives all around us. He wanted to show me a well, important to both Jews and Muslims for again having something to do with Abraham. To me it was just a big hole in the ground with stone steps leading down to the pool of water at its bottom; I didn't feel much for religious significance when suffering and persecution enveloped it on all sides. But after my friend's insistence, I dipped my fingers into the cold, clear water and asked Abraham if he *might like to help in sorting this mess out,* before we continued on our way.

At the top of the dusty path we passed a small concrete building, and my feelings soured even further as we peered into what was once apparently the girls' school for the village, now a kennel for the settlers' dogs that barked as though ravaged with rage. I haven't been able to verify whether this was indeed once a school or not, and in a sense I hope my friend was extending the truth to play out the plight of his people more. Otherwise, this was a true horror – dog mess now filling a place of learning.

We began our descent and passed back through the Portakabin, leaving the foreboding silence to return to the bustling vibrancy of H1 Hebron. I appreciated the car horns, the speakers crackling Arabic pop songs from the shops, and even the exhaust fumes clogging the air – I appreciated the presence of life, in any form.

After leaving Hebron, I returned to Bethlehem for the finest sweet sage tea I had ever had, before departing for Jerusalem where I was to stay for the next day until joining the Being Peace retreat. That night, I was locked in confusion and tried desperately to free myself through writing:

10th October
With my backpack beside me, I was again back on the bus to Jerusalem. As I knew it would be, the bus was stopped at the checkpoint back into Israel and two IDF soldiers boarded to check everyone's ID. I doubt many British ever consider how fortunate we are; our small maroon passports grant us entry pretty much anywhere (and even after our grim history of playing God with countries' independence), but to be Palestinian and prevented from travelling freely

is hard to comprehend. However, back in Jerusalem, and particularly in West Jerusalem, one can easily think, what occupation? What conflict?

Since leaving the West Bank I've been left with these recurring thoughts and I'm still suffering from them now: why the occupation? Why the ongoing conflict? I don't understand. I've missed something. What are the advantages for Israel pursuing the occupation? Okay, they get land and resources, but there are prices to pay: 1) the military budget must be sky high 2) there's constant burden of having to deal with the "Palestinian problem" 3) many around the world resent Israel for the humanitarian abuses constantly reported from the West Bank and Gaza. So why, despite these costs, do it? There must be something more to this.

I fear that in part it is a response to religious pressure; the Israeli government is at the mercy of a highly religious demographic that can unite to form a pretty persuasive vote. Hebron is a clear example of this; the settlers wanted to live next to the Temple of the Patriarchs and that Abraham well, and now they do so, with an extended family of soldiers stationed around them. Apart from this religious pressure, Israel

43

must find financial gain in taking more of the West Bank; perhaps a monopoly of trade, and the Oslo Accords have already bound Palestine to suckle from Israel like a child suckles from its mother's breast. But is this financially stable in times to come, with the cost of settling Israeli citizens in the West Bank and the ongoing questions of securing their safety and future there? Of course, I don't know.

In truth, I just don't get it. Israel is a beautiful country, strong and of great interest to people from all around the world. I think peace's only hope is for the secular state and non-radical citizens of Israel, the everyday Israeli who lives in Tel Aviv for instance, to help support its government and stop the occupation, with a united message that, "This is not good for us. It is a psychological strain on our population; our young who are not soldiers, broken into being soldiers. It is bad for our Nation's health." But then in Tel Aviv, people don't see the occupation. They do not walk down Hebron's ghostly streets, they do not talk to my young guide, learning how his daily life is affected, or see the squalid state of the refugee camps in Bethlehem. Until they do, not much change can come from within. So now I feel that insight from the international community is the key, but the Israeli people are the only ones who can take that key and use it to open the door to peace.

Killing Each Other

November 2012 – the second morning of Operation Pillar of Defense

Waking this morning to the news coming from Israel and Gaza has made these reflections seem somewhat pointless; like I've deluded myself that there has ever been another way out of the conflict, other than the path of killing each other.

The reflection I had intended to write today was entitled: Fear. I wanted it to show how fear has been so ingrained and promoted within the Israeli psyche that it now acts as one of the biggest barriers to them meeting their Palestinian neighbours, and how the constant attacks by groups like Hamas, who refuse to cease their onslaught of violent resistance, or terror, against the occupation has only served to strengthen this fear.

Hamas and anyone else who fires rockets into Israel should be held as equally responsible, along with the IDF, for the suffering and death of Palestinian and Israeli civilians that this leads to. Hamas's refusal to acknowledge Israel as a nation is one of the main preventers to peace, and its attacks against Israel only serve to give the Israeli military an excuse to launch attacks into Gaza, no matter what loss of life this leads to, adult or child.

So I cannot commence my chapter about fear today. To do so would be hypocritical on my part, as this morning I write with a real sense of fear. If the world does not act now to defuse the situation, then I fear that we are going to see the Gaza Strip become a killing field, and the fear that Israel will be left with over retaliation from other Arab states means it will strike them also, echoing the Six Day War. So activists, shopkeepers, bakers, artists, teachers and every one of us need to do all we can to close the "gates of hell" that this could very well unlock.

Another thing that troubled me during my trip to Israel and Palestine were the amount of times I heard people saying that "eventually the conflict must end". They would use South Africa as an example, or the fall of the Berlin Wall as another, and announce names like Mandela and Gandhi and say that this will happen here too.

This is troubling because we cannot wait for, or hope for, a saint-like figure to arrive and bring this suffering to an end. This will simply prolong it. Israelis, Palestinians and the international community need to be screaming out for peace, because, and despite me writing these reflections with a sense of hope, we are getting ever closer to it being too late.

Fear

At the end of the tram line in Jerusalem, you can find a viewpoint looking out across a lush green valley that leads one's gaze away from the city and towards the distant hills, blanketed by an ocean-blue sky. You will also see a sign for Yad Vashem.

Notebook in hand, and knowing that there were no religious holidays that could stop me, I began walking towards the Holocaust museum, which outlines something that I was beginning to suspect was responsible for reinforcing and prolonging today's ongoing occupation, fear.

The visitor guide that you can pick up in the museum's foyer reflects that, "The Holocaust challenges the fundamental beliefs and values of human civilization – it is a warning sign for us and future generations." I sighed in the silent, sorrowful air that drifted around the beautifully nurtured grounds. Slowly, I made my way to the first section of the museum, and the history of the Holocaust.

11th October
Yad Vashem is perhaps the most poignant, informative, beautiful and heart-rending museum I've ever been to. The history of the Jewish plight, culminating in what was to become Hitler's "Final Solution"

is clearly and powerfully presented. I think anyone who is coming to Jerusalem should see it. It is frightening to realise the speed at which one man's ideology resulted in over six million deaths. Equally frightening is that a nation bowed down to him. Before he was a dictator, Hitler was supported by the majority of his people, and once a dictator, his ideals were enforced. This is perhaps my answer as to why Israel holds an unwavering attitude with regards to its own State.

However, even at the end of the history museum, when it details the "old wooden ships" bringing the Holocaust survivors and illegal immigrants to the "Land of Israel", the Palestinians are rarely mentioned. This is not their history lesson, after all.

Halfway round, I found myself copying down some words from one of the information boards, an account from the early 1930s. To me, there are echoes of it in today's occupation. I dare not compare the two situations, but even so I see some similar methods of resource strangulation used in the West Bank. This is very sad. Another horror of the Holocaust is that the international community was indifferent to the Jews' persecution even up until the accounts of the death camps came to public attention; the Allied leaders were more preoccupied with a military victory.

I just hope that we never have to witness another museum like this, capturing the demise of the Palestinians. As powerful as it is, we should all wish that Yad Vashem did not exist, because what happened to the Jews should never have happened. But it did and I hope the museum will be received by more with the belief that this can and should never happen again, though the fear that it might is very real. I think this is at the heart of the Israeli occupation — fear. You walk around Yad Vashem and it's understandable, you cannot deny that, but fear cannot be used as an excuse to commit atrocities against others.

I left Yad Vashem with my mood heavy after visiting the children's memorial; a hall of mirrors with burning candles flickering like stars in the night sky, with the names and ages of some of the 1.5 million Jewish children who were killed during the Holocaust echoing in the background. I felt somewhat defeated, or maybe it was sadness from trying to comprehend such a harrowing history. I quickly took the tram back to Jaffa Street, and bathed in the life of this commercial section of Jerusalem.

It is important to note that the fear found

in the Israeli psyche is not to be overlooked, or dismissed. It is very real, more real even than I can ever relate.

Throughout October, and my month in Israel and Palestine, the Israel Security Agency (ISA) reported there to be 166 "terror attacks", with most of these coming from Gaza. Each one of these attacks will be portrayed in the Israeli media, penetrating the consciousness of its civilians.

During the second intifada, Israel was also reeling with the threat of suicide attacks, and their frequency and claim of life was devastating. From 2000 to 2005, more than 140 bombings were carried out in Israel, killing hundreds of civilians and instilling fear in the minds of generations to come. The barrage of attacks during this period also served to strengthen opinion for the necessity of the Separation Wall.

I carried on down Jaffa Street, where in January 2002 the first female Palestinian suicide bomber detonated a twenty-two pound explosive, killing an eighty-one-year-old man and injuring around a hundred more. What were the conditions that led this 28-year-old Red Crescent volunteer to commit such an act of terror? No-one is born a suicide bomber, they are made into one. I walked on, observing the people sipping at their frothy cappuccinos outside the coffee shops, or walking down the streets with shopping bags swaying at their sides. Today, Jerusalem is thriving; its inhabitants are free to live out their lives. But can the same be said for the Palestinians?

By the early evening I had walked to Rehavia, a green and culturally vibrant neighbourhood in central Jerusalem where I was staying for the night. Sitting outside and soaking up the ambience of Carousela, a café found on the corner of Azza and Metudela Street, I attempted to lift my mood with a cold beer, as the early dusk was already covering the paling sky. The engines of the cars on the roads hummed while waiting for the traffic lights to turn green, but in my mind all was silent except for the words that I was reading from a little booklet, which I had paid a shekel for from an orthodox Jew in a market close to Jaffa Street.

It was entitled *The Sky's the Limit* and was based on the teachings of a Rabbi Nachman of Breslov. In parts of it I thought he had some good things to say: "Without the ability to forget a person becomes constantly mired by the failures of the past, impeding any progress into the future." I drank my beer, reading back over the rabbi's words and letting the hum of Jerusalem fade into the background.

Being Peace

A month prior to arriving in the Middle East, I had the fortune to attend talks given by the renowned Vietnamese Buddhist monk, Thich Nhat Hanh. After being actively engaged against the Vietnam War, suffering the loss of many friends and fellow monks who were also working for a peaceful resolution, he has spent his life advocating a path to peace through non-violence, and, stronger still, through love.

Joining him and hundreds of others for a meditative walk amongst the architectural magnificence, or monstrosity, of La Grande Arche de la Défense in Paris had proved to be a very powerful experience. However, my thoughts were already preoccupied by my forthcoming trip to the Holy Land. How was I going to incorporate my practice into the Israel and Palestine conflict? How was I going to put, to use the title of one of Nhat Hanh's books, *Love In Action*?

Leaving London, I remember looking out of the plane's cabin window, with the clouds spread like a crumpled blanket over the Earth below. I remember thinking about the book and the ageing monk's words: "You may think that the way to change the world is to elect a new President, but a government is only a reflection of society, which is a reflection of our own consciousness. To create fundamental change, we, the members of society, have to transform ourselves."[2]

To further my chance of grappling with the conflict through a channel of inner awareness, I had registered to join a sixteen day meditation retreat offering just this, Being Peace. (Retreat is perhaps a little misleading, with the image of a group of people spending their days meditating under trees or in long grass, as Being Peace is in fact a work retreat. It is actively engaged in deepening an understanding of oneself, the conflict, and how spiritual practice can pave a union and coexistence between two warring sides. I was in for a challenging time, both physically and inwardly.)

Arriving with the group on a hillside in a neighbourhood just outside Jerusalem, we soon savoured the natural surroundings of our home for the next four nights. We let our backpacks fall from our backs and, seeking shade from the hot sun, began to learn about the people who were to share this journey into the heart of the occupation. After at least two pots of tea, we were posed the question, "Why are you here?" and I was touched by a young Israeli woman's response.

"I am here because I am afraid," she said, with the eyes of the group all settling on her. "I have grown up fearing the Palestinians, yet I have never met any. That is why I am here, to meet with my fear. I don't want to be afraid anymore."

I was suddenly aware of what it meant to have Israelis joining us, and how monumental this was for them. To be Israeli means you grow up being conditioned against the Palestinians, learning to fear them, and I can't imagine how hard it must have been for this young woman to be with us. Perhaps this is the strongest vote for peace there is, Israelis confronting their fears, seeing the occupation for what it is, and the Palestinians as people – neighbours.

This was to be our first sharing, times in which we were given the space and opportunity to recognise and voice how we felt. These reflections were to become powerful symbols of our journey together, forming a strong bond between us.

The day passed by with more introductions, spells of silence, and welcome moments of meditation. The following morning I rose early to the piercing cries of a cockerel and amidst the blossoming light of the day to come. I already had much to write:

13th October
It's around 6.30am. The grumble of traffic can be heard from the road in the valley basin, a woman is meditating in the makeshift tent to my right and a bird is chattering in the treetops. I slept remarkably well in my little dome tent.

The German man I am sharing it with doesn't snore which is always a relief.

So yesterday, after lunch and a bit of time to ourselves, we began to discuss our journey together. The picture of our time here, as best as it can be in a conflict zone, is becoming clear: tomorrow we will join with other volunteers and head to different farms to begin the olive harvest. Each year seems to change with regard to the attitude the IDF and settlers have to the presence of volunteers.

Something else that came up, and the first I've heard of it, is "anti-normalisation" on the Palestinian side. It means no longer wishing to talk to Israelis or come into contact with them, because this is seen as accepting the occupation. I can understand it, but at the same time also see it as just another barrier put up between two people.

For me, the more Israelis that see the situation and talk to Palestinians the better. I'm convinced that an answer to this occupation is for change to come from within Israel — the people — and that will only come from insight. I do not believe that the everyday Israeli has access to the full scale of the occupation, or, as it was mentioned last night, chooses to see it. Instead looking away, a survival method in dealing with the potential guilt that comes by what is occurring as a result of the country of which you are a part.

We were then given a historical overview of the situation — much of it aligned to what I had already read. Although what has been emphasised is the altering narratives that each side presents, and unfortunately this only serves to reinforce their separation. They would do well to strive towards a joint narrative — the truth. What was also interesting to learn was the propaganda used by the early Zionists: "A land without a people for a people without a land." This is how Palestine was presented, and of course it did have "a people"; the Arab population under British mandate. What the Zionists played on was that they didn't have a national identity. This argument is still used today.

The roots of this conflict are tangled and increasingly hidden beneath the soils of the past, with today's occupation growing into a bitter tree with a thick mist of distrust and deception concealing any fruits from view.

Land

The tractor grumbled forwards, pulling a trailer full of eager, slightly anxious and smiling volunteers. We were on the final road leading to our first day of harvesting; the season had commenced and the scenery around us was overcome with olive trees. The road was straight and someone called out "Roman!" over the tractor's heavy engine, before we were told that we were only to harvest to the right side of the tarmac. "The farmers might ask you to cross it," our coordinator shouted, "but *technically* we're not allowed to be there." *Why not?* Ah, that's why. Commanding the hilltop to our left was the religious Jewish settlement of Itamar, and our reason for *technically* not being allowed to be there.

This might seem strange when all of the olive trees dressing the slopes beneath the settlement belong to the same Palestinian farmers as on the opposite side of the road. How do they bring in their crop? Jumping down from the trailer, and straightening my straw hat to shield the onslaught of the hot sun, we were introduced to the farmer we had come to help.

He was a slim man with sea blue eyes and a gracious smile. I wanted to ask him how he collected his olives on the other side of the road, but this had to wait as we were all treated to our day's first sweet tea, poured from a black kettle that had been steaming away over a fire in the centre of the grove.

Sipping at the hot amber liquid, I surveyed the land to which we had come. The hills were intimidating, reaching up into the vacant blue sky, with their craggy slopes terraced into the different families' groves. They were mostly owned by Palestinians from the nearby village of Awarta. However, these lands are also harrowed by horrors. And one horror has left both Itamar and Awarta at odds, and I feel it is important to mention as the memory of it still reverberates today.

On a night in March 2011, two Palestinian men from Awarta scaled the security fence that surrounds Itamar, entered a home and murdered a Jewish family in their beds, including two children and an infant. The full account of the attack is too shocking and painful to rewrite in full. The Israeli response was severe with devastating effects on the village of Awarta and city of Nablus that were locked down by the army while the hunt for the perpetrators was felt across the West Bank.

Following this, the settlers began building more illegal outposts onto Itamar, some of which appear to have been taken down today. The Israeli Prime Minister, Benjamin Netanyahu, was even recalled as saying to the mourning families, "They shoot and we build." The farmers also began to suffer retaliatory attacks from the settlers, stopping them from picking their olives, the source of their livelihoods. This is why we were there, and what appears to have brought about the unexpected incident that I observed from up a tree, with olives landing on the plastic sheets beneath us like raindrops on a lake's surface.

I watched in amazement as two IDF soldiers, fully armed with, I presumed, purposefully big guns came over and began to shake hands with our farmer, before embarking on an everyday conversation in Hebrew about the weather no less. I was a little taken aback. Were we not there to make sure that these guys with the guns didn't shoot the Palestinians? They seemed like the best of buddies from up that tree. All was soon to become clear, mostly.

It turns out that the farmers try to maintain a good relationship with the soldiers, because if they become the victims of attacks by the settlers then often they have no-one else they can turn to for help. Being in the West Bank, the jurisdiction for settlers is a controversial and messy affair. They, after all, are Israeli citizens, who are in the confines of Israeli law. The IDF is therefore not given the authority to detain or arrest settlers, instead having to call in the Israeli police, who have a small presence in the West Bank compared to soldiers. On the flip side, Palestinians are certainly allowed to be detained, arrested, and put on trial by the IDF in a military court and under military law, far stricter and less humane than civil.

To give an example, say a group of settlers begin throwing stones at a group of Palestinians, and the Palestinians then throw stones back. The IDF would be the first to arrive and, unable to arrest the settlers, would defuse the situation by arresting the Palestinians who would then face sentencing for their crimes, while the settlers were unlikely ever to be reprimanded. This is a brief sketch of how the legal system is weighted against Palestinians, and I also want to begin to bring into awareness how lawless a settler can be.

So I continued watching the small smiles on the soldiers' faces met by the wide smiles of the farmers'. The soldiers soon left with the advice to the volunteers to mind the heat, as we're probably not used to it. A touch cynical on my part perhaps, but I found it all very staged; wondering how these same soldiers would respond if our farmer suddenly decided to throw caution to the wind, skip across the road, and commence harvesting his olives on the other side?

It all seemed too normal, as though it was not out of the ordinary to have armed soldiers walking through olive groves while families were hard at work, trying to live out their lives. But then I guess this is the West Bank; after forty-seven years, military occupation must seem pretty normal by now. Just not to me.

After some hours spent stripping the trees of their fruit, and numerous cups of sweet tea, we stopped to have lunch, which was prepared by the farmer's wife. It was a delightful spread of potatoes fried in olive oil, hummus drowned in olive oil, sour cream drenched in olive oil, with a fried egg swimming in olive oil no less, and all soaked up with plastic carrier bags full of pita bread. It was delicious. Over lunch the issue of land came up, touching on the difficulties faced by the farmers to prove that the land they harvest belongs to them.

Palestinian tradition means that there is seldom any paperwork declaring whose land is whose, with it simply being passed down through the generations. This can easily be exploited by settlers and the Israeli Supreme Court. Another story that arose was how the settlements find ways around not being allowed to expand. My attention was directed towards a distant hilltop, where a small settlement could be seen. Apparently this had been given the same name as the existing settlement and thus declared a part of it, which then brings about the question of *security*, and will inevitably result in the expansion of the original settlement's fence to include this new outpost, increasing its boundaries and grabbing more land from the Palestinians.

But the conversation didn't stop there. Once the settlement's security fence is erected there *must* be a buffer zone around it, even if this means Palestinians can't get to their trees that can end up being inside it. Another twist to this is that, according to settlers and unopposed by Israeli law, if a land is uncultivated after so many years, then it is deemed unoccupied and therefore free to lay claim to. So after not being able to cultivate their land due to the buffer zone, the farmers can find it being declared unoccupied. The security fence is then expanded, the buffer zone also and the slow process of strangulation continues.

Stories like this are all over the West Bank, but the truth behind them is hard to verify. You sometimes have to go with what you see, and it looked pretty much like this from where I was sitting, with settlements dotting the hilltops. It's also important to remember that all settlements inside the West Bank, including Itamar, are illegal in accordance to international law, but this is vehemently disputed and ignored by Israel.

"But what about the trees on the other side of the road?" I finally asked, after we had finished our lunch and were washing it down with, of all things, sweet tea. The farmer looked up towards the slopes laden with olive trees, overlooked by the white houses of Itamar. "We are not allowed to start harvesting there until the 17th, three days away," he said. "The army wouldn't give us permission any earlier." I then asked if this made the harvest difficult, and I think he almost tried to laugh but failed.

"Look," he said pointing, "you see those two people?" Squinting, I made out the form of two figures moving amongst the trees on the distant hillside. "Settlers!" he added. "By the time we're allowed to our trees, there won't be a single olive left on them." The dry manner in which he spoke gave me no reason to doubt him. I don't think he was lying to make us side with him. "Can't you do anything to protect your crop?" I asked. He didn't answer, returning instead to his family and helping to clear away lunch.

The band of volunteers, moved by his story and gracious meal, thanked him humbly before warming their fingers and attacking the next tree, searching out every last olive. Not for long mind, did someone just mention sweet tea?

The Dust of Occupation

15th October

Sitting on a bus heading out of Jerusalem, we are en route to a Palestinian village called Bel'in. It's right at the heart of the occupation. For a long time, the village was engaged in a non-violent protest against the Separation Wall that has now been constructed around its parameters, cutting people off from their olive trees.

Now the farmers have to apply for permits from Israel to pass through the wall to harvest. Apparently, out of seventy applications forty were given, and these only to the elderly or children, restrictions to adults were made on security grounds. So we are en route to help make up the numbers as the villagers only have a limited amount of time to harvest. However, without access to the groves throughout the year, the trees are likely to be in poor condition.

We've just been handed a publication by Rabbis for Human Rights, an organisation that we have teamed up with for our first days out in the olive groves. The publication argues that according to Torah holy law the occupation as it is manifesting is against

Jewish scripture. I hope to use this in my writings to come. The situation needs to be opened up to all areas of Israeli society, orthodox Jew to secular citizen.

To get to the olive grove we found it easier to travel via the Israeli side of the Separation Wall, given that the trees are now on this side anyway, but, and it's important to note, not within the Green Line. Here the wall has encroached into Palestinian land, and guess what, in the name of *security*. But this is simply a guise. The wall really secures the stolen Palestinian land that is rapidly being constructed on, establishing the settlement of Modi'in Illit.

We were soon driving through the settlement, one of the fastest expanding in the West Bank with over 45,000 residents, perhaps the largest contributing factor for the hardships suffered by Bel'in. Watching the orthodox Jews, who make up the majority of Modi'in Illit's inhabitants, standing on the pavements was something quite surreal in itself; they stared at our bus passing through their neighbourhood as though it was something from out of space. I suspected that they didn't get many outsiders. I waved at a few of them through the window, and strangely enough, only the children waved back. The adults simply held their suspicious gaze.

Suddenly the road turned to gravel and we bumped up and down along the edge of new housing units, with cranes and workmen busy finishing them while large lorries clogged the air with dust as they travelled on the road ahead. This was when I first spotted the olive grove, shrouded by high-rise buildings on one side and overlooked by the Separation Wall on the other. The trees were caged by a steel fence, penned in as though they were a threat or something to be afraid of.

The bus came to a halt and we all disembarked, taking a moment to survey the landscape and allow the two disinterested, and predominantly bored soldiers to walk slowly down from their post at the wall to check us out. "Why are you here?" the larger of the two asked. "To pick olives," was our reply, which seemed not to strike him as unusual. He began speaking into the radio pack that was held on his back like a mother holds her baby, calling in to say that, "The internationals are here again." This could not have caused much alarm to the command at the other end as they soon left to resume their post. I can't blame these two young men's lethargic manner. If I were given the responsibility of sitting in the hot sunshine while watching a concrete wall all day, I'd be pretty bored too.

So we were away; led by a spirited

Palestinian boy who had run up to meet us. Waving his arms in the air and heading back through a cut in the fence, we followed him into the olive grove, where an ageing woman and her elder son were already hard at work. The three of them had passed through the checkpoint at the wall in the morning, and were now feverishly trying to collect their olives; always under the gaze of the soldiers, the engines of the workmen rumbling, and the cheers coming from the settlement's girls' school built on the edge of the grove signalling playtime. We got to work.

The trees were a tangled web of branches spotted by ripened olives. The lack of nurture they had received showed and our small farmer, fourteen years old no less, was in command and now hacked at the trees and sawed them as best he could to get them into shape for the following year. There were no certainties as to when the family would be given permission to return to them. After just a few minutes of picking my fingers were blackened by dust, which was blown over the trees from the expanding settlement. It was the dust of occupation.

Instead of bells, Israeli schools play tunes to signal the change of lessons or breaks, similar to the tunes played by an English ice cream van. Every time I heard one of these melodies carried on the gentle breeze, I stopped to look at our young farmer, brought out of school in order to help his mother bring in their olives, with the men of the family likely to have been refused permits to come to the harvest. In that moment, I found the whole thing grotesque and deeply wrong. For the first time, I was angered by what I was seeing, and this threw me into my own inner conflict. I was meant to be able to see past my emotions, to not let them sway me into right and wrong. I did not want to take sides, because peace only comes from working with both parties. I resumed picking olives, trying to breathe out my anger, letting it be carried away on the breeze. But nevertheless questions needed to be asked.

At lunch we sat with the mother and two boys in the shade of the trees and shared another olive oil-rich meal, with delicious home-baked bread and fried aubergine. We were also joined by a young rabbi-to-be from Rabbis for Human Rights. He welcomed us and thanked us for coming to support the farmers, before asking us for our thoughts regarding the situation here. One focus for Rabbis for Human Rights is education, helping Israelis to find in the Torah a holy way that is concerned by and teaches humanitarian values to all people – Jewish and non-Jewish alike:

"Do not wrong a stranger who resides with you in your land. The stranger who resides with you shall be to you as the native among you, you shall love the stranger as yourself, for we were all strangers in the Land of Egypt: I am the Lord your God." (Lev, 19:33-34)

With this in mind, I told him that I found it incredible that the people of Modi'in Illit are predominantly religious and therefore living by the lines of the Torah, and yet do not question the suffering of their neighbours, which their choices in life have greatly contributed to. His answer was far from reassuring: "You're right, it is incredible!"

But he did point out that the population of Modi'in Illit are not the problem; they are not the same kettle of fish as the Jewish fundamentalists who have literally taken over the centre of Hebron, with or without the law on their side, be it biblical or civil. Despite being mostly orthodox, the inhabitants of Modi'in Illit are economic settlers, enticed to the settlement through government incentives and a cheaper cost of living. So this draws into question the governmental policy that undermines the occupation, and the truths that underlie this – increased land, capital, and wealth. An article published in the *New Left Review*[3] in 2006 identifies just this:

"The expansion of Modi'in Illit and similar settlements was given a further boost in the early 2000s by the construction of the 'separation wall', under shelter of Sharon's 'Disengagement Plan'. With the *de facto* annexation of the West Bank lands lying between the Wall and the pre-67 border, real-estate developers could now promise the luxury and security of gated communities to wealthy Israelis, as the local Palestinian inhabitants were barricaded out of sight. At the same time, generous government subsidies offered jobs, housing and social services unobtainable in Israel proper, a powerful magnet for those struggling to subsist. Precisely because they are not based solely on the messianic fervour of hard-line settlers but also offer answers to real social needs, these settlements are able to broaden the power base of the colonization movement, forging a powerful alliance of state, political and capitalist interests, well-off home-buyers and those suffering real hardship: large families looking for cheap housing or new immigrants dependent on government subsidies and seeking social acceptance. It is they who pay the price for the hostility that the Wall generates among those whose land it robs."

Hours later, with the last tree now bare of olives and large white sacks full of the precious fruit, the mother came around to us all personally. "*Shokran*," she kept saying, the Arabic for thank you. We smiled and helped the boys to load the sacks into the back of the bus before driving them up the hill to the wall which we could not cross, so they would have less distance to carry them.

Confusion quickly followed as the two startled soldiers were not expecting to see a herd of twenty volunteers now striding towards them. We unloaded the sacks and piled them up against the wall. The soldiers refused to allow the family to pass, telling them that they had to wait. Some volunteers contested this, saying that their homes are on the other side, and to just open the gate, but they were apparently not given the authority.

Then a very powerful thing happened, amongst the commotion of the volunteers surrounding the soldiers and arguing over the injustice of preventing people from returning to their homes, the Palestinian mother simply walked away from the group and sat silently in the shade of a concrete shelter, watching the situation before her. She had been victim to this before, and knew that no amount of arguing would let her go home any sooner. Instead, she waited peacefully, knowing that they would have to open the gate, eventually.

Reluctantly, we left them and I sat staring out of the bus' window, looking back at the mother and two boys sitting together in the presence of the two armed soldiers who had rule over their existence. The farmers smiled and waved as we left. They were grateful, but I saw the scene very differently with the wall setting the backdrop behind them. I felt the cover of my notebook in my hands, and recalled the quote I had written down from my visit to Yad Vashem, detailing an account from the early years of the Holocaust in the 1930s:

"In Eastern Europe the Nazis incarcerated the Jews in severely overcrowded ghettos, behind fences and walls. They cut the Jews off from their surroundings and sources of livelihoods, and condemned them to a life of humiliation, poverty, degeneration and death."

What was I really seeing outside my window, with dust now rising up behind the bus and impeding the view? The following day this incident would hit me, unexpectedly, in a sharing session with the group. But sitting on that bus I felt numb, with the caged-in olive grove drifting by before the settlement's school, and a group of girls who screamed and laughed as the outsiders drove past them. That night, I found a quiet spot away from the group in order to write:

15th October
Sitting back on the hillside outside Jerusalem. The light is fading and the smell of dinner is in the air. The situation here is full of barriers; the Separation Wall is a physical barrier, but it's the barriers you don't see that are the hardest to cross: religion, greed, and the human mind.

Silence

16th October

My legs are dangling from the edge of a planted terrace on what is a warm and still morning. We're having a silent period up until we set off for the West Bank and the Palestinian town where we will stay for the next few days. Before departing, we are to have a sharing discussion, giving us the chance to connect with how we feel, and also to express our opinions.

My own opinions are starting to fall away with each day I spend here. I don't see any way of countering the conflict, not until it has re-entered into Israeli debate, but the problem Israel would face if it ever did decide to give back the land in the West Bank would erupt much like an intifada; the settlers, religious ones, will never be relocated back inside Israel without a fight. If this is the case and it is doubtful that non-violence would ever be able to penetrate their closed minds, then how can we hope for an admirable, humane, and fair solution to this? It's such a mess and one that should never have been allowed to become so.

I found those periods of silence took me far deeper into myself and my feelings than I could ever have imagined. Spending parts of my summer months in a meditation centre, I have learned to appreciate silence for the depth of experience it can bring us, waking us up to life; although, my trip to the Holy Land has also shown me how silence, powerful as it is, can be incredibly destructive. A meeting with an ex-Israeli soldier had planted this seed in me. He was a representative from the joint Palestinian and Israeli organisation Combatants for Peace.

The organisation is made up by an equal number of Israelis and Palestinians who travel to both Israel and the West Bank sharing their stories with whoever will listen. The previous night we welcomed the ex-Israeli soldier, now an ageing and confident man, who had, "after seeing such senseless destruction and killing in Lebanon, changed deeply inside". He was joined by a Palestinian man who had served ten years in an Israeli jail for attacking two soldiers with a knife when he was fourteen years old. Today, and together, they use their individual experiences of the past to forge peace in the future. The organisation's slogan sums up their intent well: "Only by joining forces, will we be able to end the cycle of violence".

Towards the close of the discussion, we questioned them as to what the real barriers preventing peace were. The Israeli veteran spoke clearly: "It is the curse of *apathy* on the Israeli part, and fear on the Palestinian side."

Indifference to the situation, living out our lives instead of having to deal with the burden of confronting the pain of suffering along with our fears – this is what I took he meant by apathy. Staying silent.

But our morning's silence was coming to an end, and we all entered a large canvas tent before sitting in a circle, invited to speak in the sharing. Again, I was moved by what everyone had to say, but particularly by the words of the Israelis in the group. Reflecting on her experience of our first day harvesting, and her first time of daring to enter the West Bank, a young woman spoke about the confusion she felt inside: "I was standing there," she said, "in the middle of the olive grove and asked myself who I am supposed to be afraid of? Is it the Palestinians or the settlers? I know I'm meant to be afraid, but don't know of whom."

When it was my turn to speak, I found myself retelling the story of watching the mother we had been working with at Bil'in, and how she appeared almost to accept her fate of being controlled by the soldier at the gate, sitting peacefully before the wall while waiting to be allowed to go home. With each new word, I began to choke. I hadn't even noticed the strong emotions that this one incident had brought about in me. Later that day, and through my diary, I unlocked what it had been about seeing this that had moved me: *It was her stillness that hit me; she brought me to Palestine, whereas before I was just passing through.*

Not long after this sharing we were having another sharing, in a sense, at the Rabbis for Human Rights office in Jerusalem. The rabbi who gave up his time for us was a well-spoken and hectic man, refuelling with a coffee before sitting down with us. Working in activism is hard work, and especially against an occupation that is doing its best never to be resolved. In the hour we spent with him he opened up in me a new way of seeing the situation. Following the meeting and driving out of Jerusalem before crossing into the West Bank, with the sunshine falling on the blank white page of my notebook now open on my lap, I tried to rediscover my opinions about the occupation:

We're back on the hot bus and heading for a Palestinian town. We've just had an interesting discussion with a rabbi from Rabbis for Human Rights. It helped me to get into the heart of why I am here, and how I might be able to write about this in times to come.

This is no longer about history, whether or not what happened is right or wrong. In 1948, the Jews won a war, and these were a people who at the time had nowhere else to go. But what is now important is what the nation strives towards, a just and humane state for Palestine. There has to be a race to achieve this; if no-one can bring pressure for change inside Israel, giving Palestine a chance of life, then that's it in my mind – over. My anger at the brutality of the past is fading, and I can now see what needs to be done today. The fractures in Israeli society will make it hard, like the rabbi said, "it's been thirty years" since he last spoke to an ultra-orthodox Jew. These closed societies in Israel and in the settlements in the West Bank need to be brought into the debate; otherwise this wall between us is impenetrable.

That afternoon we arrived at Deir Istiya, an ancient stone village with a hilly landscape of olive trees and three large Jewish settlements growing around it. It's an intoxicating little place to be, with goats being herded down the streets and the call to prayer booming out of the mosque's minaret with more ferocity than being in the front row of a Led Zeppelin concert. We met our host for the week and settled into our home, sharing dinner and conversation in the small courtyard out the back. I was also given my first real taste of hope since arriving in the

West Bank.

The host's young daughter arrived and she apologised to us that she needed to practice table tennis as she had a competition the next day. We asked her how long she had been playing and she said one month, and that she preferred to play piano but couldn't have one.

Soon the *ping pong* of the practice had started from the adjoining room, and I ventured to go and watch. Inside, the sight was magical. The daughter was at one end of the table, smiling against her deep concentration, opposing her was an Israeli woman from our group, enjoying the game just as much.

Speaking out against the occupation at a conference in Jerusalem in 2011, Israeli novelist Amos Oz argues for making peace, not love. I agree with him that peace is the most important thing. But at the same time, after cheering and clapping along as the little Palestinian girl challenged her Israeli opponent's table tennis skills, I'm still convinced that we can have both – peace and love.

"Where Are You From?"

The question of identity is a challenging one, and too often stereotypes or preconceptions can be evoked, rather than meeting the individuals in question for who they really are. The longer I spent in the West Bank, the more I witnessed another barrier being erected between people: preconceived notions of who the other really is. This simply makes that wall between us larger.

On our second day of harvesting with families from Deir Istiya, I wasn't really thinking about much of anything. I was scrambling up olive trees, shaking the branches and cursing the fact that I wasn't taller after failing to reach the olives that taunted me from the treetops. I was too busy to think about the occupation. I was picking olives, and the soothing sound of them dropping onto the plastic sheets wrapped around the trunks was the only reward I needed. Hard work and repetitive as it is, olive picking remains a satisfying affair, especially when you get treated to another hummus and pita lunch, with a bowl of last year's olives pressed into a creamy thick oil on the side.

That day I had ventured out to the groves with an Israeli who had joined us for a few days on the retreat. Both he and I spent the long hot hours helping an ageing woman collect her olives, assisted by two young Palestinian chaps whom she had employed to help her. One was extremely grateful to the farmers, telling me that he joins the harvest every year. He was twenty-two years old, wearing blue stonewashed jeans and a baseball cap, and had such stamina for picking olives that he made me feel exhausted just by watching him work.

I asked him what he does outside of the harvest, remembering that it only takes place for around one month each year. "I'm looking for work," he said, before explaining that he has a degree in software programming. "It's hard to find jobs in Palestine," he added. He was the second graduate I had met who was unable to find work, and helping to make up the high unemployment rate in the West Bank. The situation is worse still in Gaza, with the UNRWA recording it to have, in 2010, one of the largest unemployment rates in the world at 45.5%.[4]

Something else I had discovered was how dependent Palestine is on foreign investment and funding. Our host back in Deir Istyia had, over dinner the previous night, mentioned that he had once opened a children's centre in the town, and it was very popular and used widely. But when Hamas were elected in Gaza, America stopped giving money to projects there and the school was forced to shut down. One thing is clear, if Palestine is ever to sustain a future then it will have to be able to stand alone, but this is not an easy thing to achieve as the World Bank[5] points out:

"A quarter of the Palestinian population lives in poverty, with rates in Gaza being twice as high as that in the West Bank. [...] The PA is facing a grim fiscal situation. With a higher than expected budget deficit and donors' expected support in 2014 less than last year's amount, the PA is trying to reverse the situation through steps to raise domestic revenues and control expenditures. A dynamic private sector can generate the sustainable growth needed. However, restrictions put in place by the Government of Israel continue to stand in the way of potential private investment. Access to Gaza remains highly controlled and much of Area C, comprising 60 percent of the West Bank, is inaccessible to Palestinians."

We continued picking and I wondered where these olives would end up, either pickled or pressed, and what growth, if any, this would bring to the Palestinian economy.

With the sun commencing its final decent, carpeting the sky in many shades of orange, we helped the two young Palestinians to lug the white olive-filled sacks to the roadside. Our day of picking was over, but we still had an unpleasant experience to come, and one that this occupation can bring forth, being faced with the question: *Where are you from?*

My Israeli co-volunteer and I were offered a lift back to town by a relative of the farmer we had been helping. He was a middle-aged man wearing smart clothes, heavy aftershave and told us that he worked in a nearby city. We hopped into the back of his car, thanking him for the ride and saying hello to his black-veiled wife sitting in the passenger seat. We were soon driving away from the olive grove with the sun finally setting in the reflection of the rear-view mirror.

This is when I noticed our driver's eyes in the glass, examining us. "Where are you from?" he asked, turning down his funky Arabic music playing on the stereo. "England," I replied promptly, thinking his questions as nothing out of the ordinary. "And you?" he said, now barely concentrating on the road ahead as he examined my friend in the mirror. "Israel," he eventually said. "Ah, but you believe in peace right?" the driver enquired, holding the wheel tightly and appearing to have found a new focus for the journey home: giving a message.

Deciding that this was slightly unnecessary, considering my co-volunteer clearly believed in peace for the simple fact of his being there to pick olives with this man's relative, I thought I'd try and push the conversation on a little (not enjoying awkward moments, especially when I'm stuck in a moving car with one.) "Were you born in the town?" I asked him, before quickly biting my bottom lip. He slowed the car so he could meet with our eyes in the mirror. "I was born on these lands, as was my father, and my grandfather before him," he said slowly and purposefully.

My Israeli friend nodded, as did I, looking out the window for our drop-off point. I wish I could write that this was the end of it, but after closing the car doors behind us and thanking our driver for his kindness, we began to walk to our house in the centre of the town to reconvene with the rest of the group, who had all been out harvesting the day away too.

Arriving at the door, we were suddenly jumped upon by a group of children, who were all smiles and excitement as they wanted to shake hands with the strangers. "Hello! Hello! Where are you from?" they cheered. "England," I said, now laughing with them. "England! England!" they said to each other, all taking it in turns to high five me. "And you, where are you from?" they then asked my friend. "Israel," he replied quietly. The children instantly stepped back, as if being suddenly confronted by the Bogeyman, and began whispering amongst themselves: *Israel! Israel!*

My friend entered the house and I stayed

for a few minutes more with the children, talking about – that's right – football teams. Inwardly however, I was thinking how sad it was that by the age of eight these children had already come to fear Israel. Instead of being able to see my co-volunteer for the genuinely nice person that he is, they were scared and shied away from him. This is the fault of adults, both Israeli and Palestinian, for each side caters in some way for the passing down of hatred and fear.

Later that evening, the group took time to share and reflect on how the day had gone. The Israeli I had been working with responded to the things he had encountered, expressing his hopes that one day he can be "seen for who he is, and not for where he comes from." This is the same for anybody, not just those from Israel, for we are all more than an overused and often misleading characterisation.

When writing a story, perhaps I'll think about a protagonist in this way, but not when I want to form a relationship with a neighbour, and especially when so much is at stake by our engagement – our children's future.

A Beautiful Day...

19th October

A donkey is braying in the distance, birds are singing in the fruit trees, and the dawn is almost at its end. I'm sitting on a concrete wall on our second-floor balcony. On the road below, a Frenchman from the group is patting down his body and doing some stretches. He's a strong and rugged-looking man, with grey stubble, a shaven head, and a gentle demeanour set within his rigid cheekbones. I found out yesterday that he was born in 1941; he looks good for being over seventy. Now one of the Englishmen has also joined in, stretching out his body beside him. I wonder what the Palestinian villagers must think of this scene.

Perhaps I should be there too, stirring my mind and body for the day ahead. If it's anything like yesterday then I will encounter much movement today, picking olives from 8am until 5pm.

Sitting here, I've a wide panoramic view of the sky, distant hills and my questions before me. I've a feeling my questions are always going to be one of the biggest parts of my time here.

Not long after this entry, and following a

meditation accompanied by the mosque's rapturous call to prayer, we were en route to the olive groves. On that day I was sent out with one of the Israeli women from our group; the one who had moved me by her honesty in sharing the fear she felt for being in the West Bank, and the same one who had been having such fun playing table tennis with our Palestinian host's daughter. Sitting in the back of the taxi, we watched the sun rising over the sea of olive trees that flooded the landscape all around us. Rubbing my hands together, I warmed my fingers for the picking to come.

Stepping out of the taxi on a new tarmac road, leading towards one of the Jewish settlements a kilometre or so ahead, we waited to find out where we would be working. The taxi driver sounded the horn two times before turning in the road and racing back towards Dier Istyia. We waited with bottles of water in our hands and rising smiles on our faces as a small boy burst out from the groves and began running towards us, waving his hands in the air.

"Hello! Come, come, quickly," he said, spinning on his heels and leading us into the maze of trees over the rocky red soil to meet his family, and the farmers we had come to help for the day. It was a family of seven: mother and father, the father's younger brother, and then their four children; a twelve-year-old girl, the eleven-year-old boy who had come to meet us, a three-year-old girl who could smile her way to anything and a fifty-day-old baby, sleeping in its cot under the shade of a tree. We all said hello to each other, and then got to work circling a tree that was laden with bruised-purple olives.

English was not a language we could share, so I became the happy observer as my Israeli co-volunteer and the father farmer began talking in Hebrew. It is quite common for Palestinians to speak Hebrew, as there is a large labour force of Palestinians who are given permits to enter Israel for work. There are many grey areas surrounding this issue, particularly workers' rights, low wages and the lack of revenue that this brings the Palestinian infrastructure. In reality it's simply a case of people going where the work is – they will do what they have to do to survive and to feed their families. Something I always struggled to stomach was going through the settlements in the West Bank and seeing Palestinians employed as construction workers – it's a strange thing to be helping to build the very thing that is stripping you of your own land and future independence.

Back at the grove, I had somewhat forgotten about picking olives as I was having too much fun playing with the children. All day long, the little boy would call out my name,

"Matthew, Matthew!" and wave a black bucket as his role was to collect all the fallen olives that had bounced from the mats into the dusty soil. I joined him and soon he wanted me to teach him English by lunchtime. I told him that this was *ambitious*, which he agreed with, not knowing the word's meaning. "You teach me English," he said again. "Talk! Talk!"

"How old are you?" I asked. He looked at me, dropping the bucket to count his fingers. "Eleven, eleven years, I am eleven years!" he declared proudly. Our lesson continued for some time until I felt a tug at my neck as his three-year-old sister was pulling at my camera. "Give, give," she said softly in Arabic, before wanting me to take pictures of her swinging from the trees.

I easily forgot about the real reason for our being there, to prevent the family from not being able to harvest by soldiers or settlers, and instead I was enjoying the day for what it was – a group of strangers coming together to pick olives. How easily this wall between us would fall down if only we could all engage in such a simple act of solidarity.

Following a lunch like nothing I ever imagined possible to create in an olive grove, stuffed vine leaves and courgettes, we rested together and shared tea. "Give, give," the little girl whispered into my ear in Arabic, again tugging at my camera and soon becoming the day's official photographer.

89

Sipping at his tea, her uncle, nearing thirty with a relaxed nature, questioned me over my thoughts about the situation in Palestine. I always found this a hard thing to comment on, especially to Palestinians and Israelis, not knowing enough about the conflict except how complicated it is. I said it must be incredibly difficult for them, and how I have been so very lucky to have lived a free life. He nodded before meeting with my eyes. "Our situation is very bad," he said simply. It was the cold directness in which he had voiced these words that told me how much the occupation had ground the life out of him. He didn't say why it was bad, or what needs to be done to make it better. He just returned to his tea, drinking it slowly.

Towards the end of the day, we were joined by two other members from the group and we all picked away happily, sharing tales of how spoilt we had been for food, and episodes of falling out of trees. As the sky turned amber, we helped the family to hide the white sacks of olives we'd picked under branches for them to collect the following day, and soon made our way back up to the road.

Sitting on the roadside the two sisters were giggling to each other when an army Jeep appeared around the corner, coming from the settlement. On seeing it approach the children sprang to their feet and ran towards their mother. Saddened by what I had seen, I watched the Jeep drive by us, and the moment quickly passed with no-one saying anything.

On our bus back to town, I was left watching the deepening sky and sinking sun outside my window, questioning how it had come to pass that a three-year-old girl already has an association of fear with Israel, and enough to cause a physical response at seeing an army Jeep. This is yet another tragedy in a region where it seems tragedies have become the staple of being alive.

Opening Our Hearts

20th October

The thud of the Frenchman slapping his body in his morning warm-up ritual is coming from behind me; birds are filling the air with their calls, and a wasp has taken the trouble to fly up to the second-floor balcony to hover around me. I'm not really sure what I'm to write. I know I'm writing to keep the connection I have sought to make with my pen, but it doesn't always mean we have words to share.

The young Israeli from the group has just returned from her morning walk. It's still only 5.45am, but early mornings feel normal now and it's quite light. I really admire her; it's so powerful to see the way she talks to the farmers, and plays with the children just as she did in the olive grove yesterday. If only more Israelis and Palestinians could open themselves up to this kind of engagement. It's hope in the present, and in a present when not much hope is there.

This entry was followed by another long strenuous day picking olives and then a much needed silent day, where the group engaged in many meditation sittings and a sharing, broken in the afternoon by a fascinating trip to an olive press.

I had been grappling all day with this idea of how to get more Israelis and Palestinians to meet each other, to break down this wall between them, in order to see each other for the victims that they both are. They are both victims of hatred, fear and leaderships that insist on taking them further and further into the belief that the only solution to ending this suffering is killing each other. But how can this ever be changed?

21st October

Lots of meditation so far today with four sittings this morning alone. I'm still wavering in them, my mind's a natural wanderer. We've an hour before our next sit so I thought I'd pick up my pen.

The girls' school must have finished for the day as a stream of girls in green uniforms are walking up the road below the balcony; some wearing hijabs on their heads and some not. Despite being fairly traditional, with alcohol not for sale anywhere in the town, there is still quite a diverse population of religious and secular. Now a cool wind is pushing against me; it's most welcome as it's another baking hot day.

Despite it being Sunday the children are at school and the adults at work. The Muslim holy day is on Friday, and therefore Sunday is just another normal working day, much like in Judaism. It would normally take some adjusting to, but I don't really have a concept of days or weeks at the moment and especially not of seasons; we are nearing November and still touching thirty degrees.

Meditate as I might, I could not pinpoint a path to peace. Helplessness is something that all activists will have to face in working for Israel and Palestine. But this just means we have to come together, and work harder to see this helplessness as a strength, because it shows us just how passionately we care for the very thing that we are fighting for. Every time I was overcome by a sense of helplessness, I would turn to the Israelis who were with us, watching them also meditating and working for peace within themselves as well as for their neighbours. This was all the inspiration I needed to come out of my meditations believing that peace has a real chance, despite still being none the wiser as to how to help make it triumph.

At the olive press, and slightly relieved to be moving after sitting cross-legged for much of the day, we were guided by the foreman through the complex nature of first washing the olives in hot vats of water, then crushing them into what looked like a green pâté, before a man seated on a plastic chair finally opened a tap for the golden reward of pure pressed olive oil to drip out.

Children crowded around us, and outside the press the workers indulged us with cups of fizzy drinks as the sun once again treated us to a beautiful departure, setting over Deir Istiya to leave behind a burning-ember sky. We drank our drinks, burping with the bubbles and laughing with the children; Israelis, Palestinians, and Europeans together – all opening our hearts to each other.

A Question Before a Storm

22nd October

A long day in the olive groves today; we worked with a farmer along with his wife and elderly mother. Their trees are beside the settlement of Revara, and three days ago, members of our group were approached by soldiers in full camouflage saying that they were not allowed to be there. Of course they were, and after many phone calls the soldiers had to concede and sneaked back off into the olive grove to continue their secret mission.

Fortunately, today passed by undisturbed and we picked lots of olives. We were joined by three women from The World Council of Churches; it's an interesting organisation that seeks to unite all of the different denominations of Christianity, despite their differences. I thought that this is not a bad concept, and perhaps we would do well to also have a World Council of Humanity.

I have skipped evening meditation to sit here writing this; it felt like a good thing to do only five minutes ago, but now I'm not really sure where it's going. I feel unknown to myself at the moment, which is a little strange as going on a

96

A morning during Sukkot celebrations, large numbers of Jews pray in front of the Western Wall. The Temple Mount is the holiest site in Judaism.

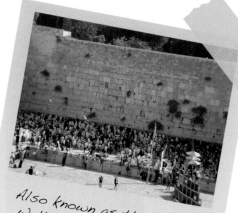

Also known as the Wailing Wall, men and women pray separately. Here, women are to the right of the picture and men to the left.

An Israeli flag
hangs from a
window in the
Old City of East
Jerusalem.

Jewish market stalls in
East Jerusalem selling
religious paraphernalia.

The Dome of the Rock, with its golden roof and intricate mosaics, is a testament to Islamic architecture.

A Palestinian flag flies in the evening breeze on a hilltop outside Bethlehem.

A covered market
offers a wide variety
of produce in the
heart of Bethlehem.

An olive farmer resting and
drinking sweet tea.

Children in Deir Istiya
offering smiles and
peace signs.

One tree can produce
hundreds of olives and
this farmer is busy
picking her valuable crop.

Lunchtime in the olive groves
and a chance to sample
Palestinian cuisine.

Helping her son to harvest, this elderly woman's trees are now beside an Israeli settlement. Many farmers in the West Bank fear they will be restricted access to their groves.

H2 Hebron is Israeli controlled. The tarmac road is for settlers, permitting them to drive. The narrower pavement is for Palestinians, forbidden to drive or access parts of the city.

H2 Hebron - Shops welded shut and Palestinians expelled from their homes, an army patrolled ghost town now exists in the middle of the city.

In construction, the Israeli West Bank Barrier (referred to by many Palestinians as the Apartheid Wall) isolates these homes in al-Walaja as the wall fully encloses the town.

Barbed wire replaces concrete in some sections of the Israeli West Bank Barrier.

A red rose placed on rubble in
al-Walaja.

Many of the delicacies
produced in the Holy
Land can be found in
Carmel Market in
Tel Aviv.

Hummus in
the ancient
port city of
Jaffa,
Tel Aviv.

Palestinian flag
placed next to a
spring at Wadi Kana.

Israeli soldiers observe and protect the
parks authority which is in Wadi Kana
to mark olive trees to be uprooted.

A tree in Wadi Kana
marked for uprooting.

Morning of the uprooting
at Wadi Kana, the army
leaves as farmers go to
inspect their loss.

The ancient town of Deir Istiya.
Mules and donkeys are used
to carry heavy sacks of olives.
Infrastructure in the West
Bank is poor and rubbish is a
common sight in rural towns and
communities.

meditation retreat is often meant to strengthen your understanding of your being. Perhaps it's just a process of stripping off the layers of identity that we all ascribe to ourselves.

After dinner, our group facilitator, an Israeli, told us about a matter that has been affecting her for the past three weeks. A Palestinian family here in the town has a problem; their eight-year-old daughter has leukaemia and is in need of treatment in Israel, because there are not the facilities to help her in Palestine. There was a long process of getting her into a hospital, with the Palestinian Authority paying for her treatment in the end, and now her father has been refused a permit to enter Israel, so our group facilitator has been helping him to try and obtain one. It's so desperately painful that human beings have fallen so low that a father is prevented from being at his sick daughter's side. I am stumbling over a question that is but a whisper in my mind, an echo: what is humanity?

*

... Just returned from sitting on the balcony; a lightning storm is shivering through the night sky in the distance. I couldn't find an answer to my question, but found myself instead reflecting on another incident from today. It felt strange to sit on the roadside outside the settlement after collecting olives. On the road, Palestinians and Israelis were all driving by, going about their day. It shows that the two people can live without a wall between them.

I'm really tired and going to turn over my question while waiting for sleep to take me. It's haunting to think that the little Palestinian girl who is sick is only a year younger than my niece. I don't know how I would respond if she were ever ill and someone put a barrier up to prevent me helping her. This girl's family must be suffering terribly.

The Settler and the "Holy" Settlement of Shilo

23rd October

Sitting back on the balcony outside our home in the Palestinian town of Deir Istiya; a woman from the group is at the other end watching the early morning fade into the increasing grumble of tractors trundling down the road. The lightning storm failed to bring any rain and it looks like it's going to be a clear day, beautiful in fact. I slept deep all night, not even woken by the 5am call to prayer that normally shakes you from your dreams as it echoes through the concrete walls. Olive harvesting is tough-going. I can't imagine doing it for longer than a month.

So we are leaving Deir Istiya today and heading to Jerusalem; it will be nice to be camping back on the hillside. But before we arrive there we are going to visit a settlement along with a settler who has agreed to talk to us. I'm going with the intention of listening, and I will have to see what questions arise from that.

Following a silent morning, allowing us to

process our time with the farmers in Deir Istiya, we were back on the bus and en route to the settlement of Shilo, seen by its inhabitants and the government of Israel to be built on State land, whereas the international community condemns it as illegal for its situation inside the West Bank, outside of the Green Line and therefore on Palestinian land. Would it surprise you to then learn that this site, like the downtown settlements of Hebron, also holds holy significance in Jewish biblical history? No, me neither.

Arriving at the settlement you pass by a little glass booth that has a private security guard inside, appearing almost as bored as the soldiers given the task of staring at a concrete wall all day. And then you are following a black tarmac road past the whitewashed houses and tended green lawns as well as colourful play parks; Shilo feels like driving through the set of *Desperate Housewives*, or any other street in American suburbia. I peered out of my window, questioning how this could still be the West Bank, and what on earth made this place holy.

So back we must go into history, helping us to solve the puzzle of the present. According to the Hebrew Bible, during the Exodus from Egypt the Divine Presence was said to reside in a portable dwelling place known as the Tabernacle. This meant the

Israelites could carry it with them on their journey and eventual return to the Promised Land. However, before the construction of the First Temple of Solomon in Jerusalem in the 10th century BC, the Tabernacle was placed in Tel Shilo, making it a pilgrimage site for hundreds of years for Jews and resulting in today's revered archaeological site that the settlement of Shilo has been built next to. But perhaps the settler could better explain his decision for being there, if religious reasons alone weren't sufficient.

We pulled up outside a red-bricked bungalow, built on the top of the hill with a view over the vast valley basin, which has been turned into some kind of field for commercial crop production, with big black irrigation pipes snaking across it. In a line, we walked up the garden path and towards the smartly dressed gentleman who was standing on the porch.

Our settler was an ageing man, sixty or so, with a soft smile and welcoming manner, showing us into his home and presenting cups of water and little pieces of chocolate gateaux. I was already sitting on the edge of my seat, sensing the tension I knew I would find and secretly fought to suppress it. I wasn't interested in niceties; I solely wanted to know how he reasoned to himself that settling in the West Bank was justifiable, and particularly how he supported this decision through his religion.

The meeting with the settler began. He gave us an introduction to the recent and ancient history of Shilo, touching on what I have just told you about the site of the temporary temple, before alluding to the triumph and great satisfaction of establishing today's settlement in the late 1970s. He spoke for some time not really touching on the Palestinians, but soon we were offered the chance to ask questions. The discussion was instantly brought to today's reality, and the subject of occupation.

In talking about the "Arabs" he was visibly saddened, if not a little burdened by having to go by this route, but he answered us honestly, and I respected him for this. He mentioned how at one time the relationship between the settlement and the nearest Palestinians village used to be 'okay', but then during the first and second intifada the settlement was attacked and since then there has been no interaction between the two. Instead of a wall, a fence has been erected between them, both physically and mentally.

It upset me that he always reverted back to the tragedy of the Palestinian people being a result of them being let down by their political leadership, with a refusal to recognise Israel as an entity and accepting its sovereignty. This means that in a sense, until the leaders of Palestine say otherwise, nothing can be done about this situation. It's not Israel's problem. However, in the meantime, it will simply indulge itself in a rapid expansion of settlements, and then wonder, or more likely not, why there is no apparent lust for peace in the Palestinian psyche, when all they see are yellow diggers, lined by soldiers, digging up their land and building homes on it. For me this is a two-way tragedy, promoted equally by the Israeli leadership and sustained by its greed.

But I bit my lip, instead listening to him introduce a hypothetical reason for Israel being unable to allow Palestine its independence: "The risk of Palestine having its own State is too great for the Israeli people," he declared. "What if they had an army? What if they acquired large wealth, weapons? What if they decided to use them against us?" This was one *what if* too many and I asked him if this meant that fear was an acceptable justification for the continual oppression and suffering inflicted on the Palestinian people. He looked at me and asked simply, "Do you mean politically or morally?" I almost choked on my word, "Both!"

He took a breath and sat back in his chair, weighing up my question before explaining that both people suffer. Personally, this was the first time where I truly felt that the words he was saying were coming from deep inside him. We all have a mind, and even if you have God on your side, you won't sleep easily if there is even a touch of doubt about the choices you have made in life, particularly if other people suffer because of them.

He told me that he didn't see the oppression that I had mentioned. But then I guess he doesn't take many day trips out into the West Bank, as I could recommend Hebron as a place where not only could he pay his blessing to the patriarchs, but also have a tour of both oppression and persecution if he would like to. In fact, if we had more time, I would have liked to ask him many more questions about theology, and how the Torah is read in light of the modern-day State of Israel. Does it really align to this Biblical Land that we read about in scripture?

But the meeting had to come to its end, and I was both grateful to him and also frustrated that he had finished by deeming the settlements in the West Bank to be, "The first line of defence of the State of Israel." I was staggered, for I see the settlements in the West Bank to be one of the largest contributing factors to unachievable peace. How can you negotiate a truce with someone when you are visibly stealing from them? We left with me feeling unsatisfied, like I had deluded myself that we might be able to plant a seed of insight into this man, but instead he simply watched us leave, waving from his porch. Silently, we drove back out of Shilo, bursting out of the settlement's bubble to breathe once again within the vast rugged and rocky land of the West Bank.

23rd October

Before leaving the settler, a member of the group took to him with an analogy: there is a pizza on the table between two people, said to be owned by both of them. And while the difficult questions about who owns what are answered, the bigger and stronger of the two has already started eating the pizza. Despite its simplicity, this reflects quite well today's situation.

But for now I'm sitting here on a hillside on the edge of Jerusalem; the sun has said farewell and dropped from the sky, and the wind is playing in the tall reed-like plants before me. Now this is holy.

Breaking the Silence

I thought I'd seen it all already. There couldn't be anything more harrowing then seeing the empty streets, the shops wielded shut and the sombre faces of the Palestinians as they were searched by a soldier for the simple crime of returning to their homes. Yet I thought wrong about Hebron. Unfortunately, there was yet more to see.

Seated in a large bus full of internationals I returned to the largest city in the West Bank with the organisation Breaking the Silence. The organisation was established in 2004 by a group of soldiers who had served in Hebron, and who felt compelled to speak out about their experiences in the Occupied Territories. Today, over 700 testimonies have been compiled, bringing perhaps one of the strongest voices into Israeli society, revealing the true nature of the occupation through the accounts of serving soldiers. But, still, does Israel see? Will it listen to its own children?

"As long as there is no political will to change the situation, this is how it is going to look," our guide, and ex-soldier, told us as the bus tore through the West Bank, with the large settlement of Kiryat Arba filling the horizon before us, also to be our first stop.

Kiryat Arba has a population of over 7,000 and is the largest of all the settlements found in and around Hebron. It also has a park with a tomb in it for a man named Baruch Goldstein. Why on earth were we stopping to see a tomb to an American-born Jew, who had lived in this settlement? I'm afraid this story makes my stomach turn some, and even more so as this man is now remembered and his grave frequently visited by people who praise his actions in life. So the tour of Hebron began; our guide led us to the tomb and explained why Goldstein is a legend to the people of Kiryat Arba.

In 1994, dressed in his army uniform and carrying a rifle, Goldstein entered the Tomb of the Patriarchs in central Hebron and began to open fire on the Muslims who were at prayer inside. He was able to kill twenty-nine Palestinians and wounded another 125 before he was wrestled to the ground and beaten to death. So tell me again, why has this mass-murderer now got his own tomb in a green park in an illegal settlement in the West Bank?

To some, Goldstein's actions were pure and true to the Nation of Israel. However, mainstream orthodox Jews denounced him, and the Israeli government at the time was quick to condemn the attack. But still, this does not change the fact that I was looking down upon a white stone tomb, with pebbles placed on it showing that it had recently been venerated. Who would revere this man?

Ultra-extremists, be they settlers or not, and people who I find it hard to be sympathetic towards.

Before we start to get into a debate about anti-Semitism over my disgust with the choices and actions of the settlers who have been taking over parts of Hebron for themselves, no matter the effect that this has on the Palestinian inhabitants or who dies along the way, I will make a brief statement: I am not anti-Semitic. I side with the orthodox Jews in mainstream Israeli society who condemn this atrocity, and I side with morality against anyone, extremist or not, when it comes down to how we treat one another, and the way we live out our lives.

Unfortunately many settlers (though not all) in Kiryat Arba respect what Goldstein did, and these are the very people who will soon put up the biggest barrier to ever finding peace between Israel and Palestine. Presently Israel's right-wing government isn't fussed about peace, because it's having a splendid time taking all it can from the West Bank while the international community dithers over what to do about it. But one day, if the Israeli people choose to see what's happening and decide peace is something worth achieving, it will elect a government that will work for peace. But there is going to be a big problem preventing peace and a two-state solution, through the radical settlers who have commanded parts of the West Bank, supported by the government or not, and what their reaction will be.

They will not share this space, they will not relinquish this land they have stolen, because their religious convictions will not allow them to, because they have deluded themselves that scripture must be followed absolutely without even attempting to fit this into a present-day awareness of cause and consequence. If these settlers in the centre of Hebron are truly acting in accordance with God, then God is not someone I ever want to meet. And that's sad for me to admit, because I had always seen God as life and love – inside us all.

Already feeling deflated after only the first stop, we got back on the bus and began to head down the H2 controlled roads into central Hebron, stopping before the Jewish entrance to the Tomb of the Patriarchs.

Leaving the bus, I observed two soldiers firing a little toy up into the air, obviously bored from standing before the steps leading up to the tomb all day. One chased after it as it tumbled back down to earth; he would have aroused the image of a schoolboy in a playground, if he wasn't wearing full army dress along with a pistol at his waist. So we had arrived at the sickening tourist attraction that was downtown Hebron. Take a deep breath and let the tour begin.

We began by passing down a street that had been split into two, a wide section and a narrower one. We continued down the wider section with a small flow of Palestinians walking up the narrow one. Our ex-soldier explained that many roads in central Hebron had been given different categories; Palestinians were not allowed to walk down some, and they could walk but not drive down others, which Israelis could drive down. Hence why our section was wider. Occasionally a car displaying an Israeli number plate passed us. This I have to point out is again done in the name of *security*. Every action the IDF takes which is backed by the Israeli government is excused by this one word: *security*.

Breaking the Silence was formed to reveal the unknown of the occupation, and this is what our guide proceeded to do. He stopped us in an empty street, the shops again barred shut with a soldier sitting on a rooftop overlooking us. It was explained that what was happening in Hebron was all done with the objective of making Isreal's presence felt.

Shortly into our tour, visiting streets that had been blocked off by big slabs of concrete, we were learning about the once-thriving chicken market, now another place inaccessible to the Palestinians that had once lived in and owned the shops around the area. At this point a hoard of army Jeeps began to park opposite us, with another group of people heading our way – another tour.

Most days, the settlers of downtown Hebron provide tours to Jewish people interested in the Biblical significance of Hebron or even considering becoming a part of the settlements themselves. This tour was for American Jews and I can't lie, they weren't that pleased to see us. Their tour leader quickly told them that our tour was "Anti-Israel!" and didn't stop to learn that it's in fact nothing of the sort and truly against the occupation, and in the long run seeks to help Israel by working towards a future that no longer sees its children forced into committing acts of inhumanity. But then this settler was too preoccupied with what the chicken market had been over 2,000 years ago to think about the squalid shit-hole it had been turned into. Did he actually look upon the same concrete and barbed wire as us, or was he so blinded by his faith and convictions that even persecution could be made to look holy?

We walked away from them with one American kindly shouting back at us to, "Go back to England and the IRA!" The army escort went with them and we were left in the silent vacuum of the empty streets, amazed by what had just happened. Arriving back at the Portakabin that I had previously passed through with my Palestinian guide on my first trip to the city, I felt overwhelmed with helplessness again. Turning to the hill where he had first shown me the girls' school that had since become a kennel for the settlers' dogs, I thought about the extent of the evil at work here. Hebron is the closest I've ever come to seeing it, and without organisations like Breaking the Silence then we never would.

After walking along the streets observing the Palestinians walking soberly past us, while the Israeli settlers drove stern-faced in their cars, we arrived at the end of our tour with a white stone building on one side of the road, and an old stone building on the other, with all the windows and doors covered by cages. This white stone building belonged to settlers and opposite it the Palestinian household had felt the need to protect their windows with cages. Why was this? What had been thrown at this house in the past? The ex-soldier explained how the IDF finds it hard to police the settlers, they have no jurisdiction over them, and settlers can feel at ease to throw things at the homes of Palestinians, and taunt them with anything that will help them to leave sooner.

Clenching my notebook in my hand, I found myself drawing on the wisdom of the renowned mystical scholar, Andrew Harvey, whose book, *The Hope*, outlines a path out of our global crises through Sacred

Activism. I questioned how I too could turn the anger that I felt after my tour in Hebron into compassion. At the time, with the graphic sights and sterility all around me, I didn't think I ever could. But weeks later, I no longer feel this anger towards the settlers, for they are more lost than any of us, and it will take the greatest compassion to help them to see it. What's happening in Hebron is immoral, and I invite anyone who doubts me to join a tour provided by Breaking the Silence.

25th October

The fire is cindering in the pit before me; the night sky looms overhead, touchable even. It was nice to cook for the group tonight and return to normality after visiting Hebron. It's honestly like walking onto a Hollywood movie set; the problem being that this film is real. It's sterile and full of welded-up shops, soldiers and absurdities.

I really will find it hard to give words to Hebron. It's surreal and not comparable to anything I've ever seen before. So for tonight I will lay down my pen and watch these burning embers instead, and the lightning storm silently approaching in the distant black sky.

Cut Off

The stories are all we have. They're all we're left with, once the dust of occupation settles, and white buildings behind a big concrete wall now stand on land that you once held the sincere belief belonged to you, with the flickering memory of a home you shared with your family. What will you do? People tried to help you, they said what is happening here is wrong; they petitioned on your behalf, they protested against the injustice. But still, there you now sit, on a rock in an olive grove looking around at the barricade that now surrounds your existence. You're penned in, caged like an animal and treated no better. So again, what will you do? Your livelihood has been snatched away before you, your land built on and your dignity as a fellow human being diminished and considered worthless. So please, tell me what will you do? Where can you go? You have nothing left, except this story perhaps. But what good will that do you now?

This story is set in the Palestinian town known as al-Walaja, soon to be completely encircled by the Separation Wall, and its inhabitants have, despite the ongoing support from Israeli and international activists, been unable to stop this absurd nightmare from being implemented. Joining a co-ordinator from Engaged Dharma and Friends of Walaja, two Israeli groups that work for a peaceful and non-violent resolution to the occupation, we ventured to the outskirts of the town, stopping before an incomplete section of the wall. In a cold wind, signalling the approaching autumn, we walked around looking towards the sprawl of Jerusalem in the distance.

I guess I don't have to explain that *security* is the excuse for having to build the wall in almost a 360-degree path around Walaja. Every other inhumane action that Israel does in the West Bank is excused by this word, *security*. So the strangulation of Walaja should be no different, and of course it's not. Also wrapping Walaja on all sides are three settlements, the reason for the chosen path of the wall, with the settlement of Har Gilo built right at the entrance of the town. Unsurprisingly, the sound of construction was also carried on the wind, as the settlements expand, laying further claim to the land before the world wakes up and realises it could possibly have prevented this. I fear it's too late now to stop the settlements, but still the story must be told because people are suffering, and something has to be done.

Crossing our arms to hold in our warmth we soon headed into the town, to meet with a gentleman who agreed to talk to us. He grew vegetables but explained how the town has been suffering water shortages for the past couple of years, and the struggle to try and fix this without having a real body that they can turn to. What was then outlined was the difficulty of building new homes in their own town. To do so they have to apply for planning permission through Israel and it was quickly explained that most requests are never responded to, and the others simply rejected. So this means that the majority of homes in the town are constructed without planning and Israel will occasionally send in bulldozers and have them destroyed. The families, having nowhere else to go, will promptly rebuild them. One house can be rebuilt and destroyed many times. I looked back up to the hilltop with all the settlement's homes being built without restriction. I breathed out my anger, questioning how this is ever justifiable.

On one side of Walaja, a barbed wire fence has been erected instead of the wall; this was done after lobbying about the environmental importance of this region. The silver wire glimmered in the sunshine that broke through the clouds, as it traced the hillside to as far as the eye could see. But Walaja is not the only town at risk of being affected by the route of the Separation Wall. We were soon back on our bus and now heading for another town 5km west of Bethlehem, Battir.

Arriving in Battir, you are greeted by the

most beautiful dress that nature could find to adorn herself in. The hillsides are rich with varying shades of green, and the fertile soils home to an abundance of cultivated crops fed by natural springs that flow into them using the irrigation system that was installed by the Romans. The Separation Wall is planned to be built at the bottom of the valley, cutting Battir off from around 30 percent of its ancestral land. What is equally sad about this is not just the devastating effect this will have on the town's sustainability through food production, but also the tragic consequences to Battir's blossoming infrastructure.

I was uplifted to listen to the plans and projects that are taking place in Battir. Despite the difficulty of living under occupation, residents are going out there and doing things. We learnt about the eco-tourism projects: the guest house soon to open overlooking the lush valley, and the footpaths being made to allow visitors to be amongst the natural wonder surrounding Battir. All of these will be ruined by the presence of the concrete scar that is the Separation Wall. Battir is still one place that has a chance; the construction of the wall has been halted and is now in dispute in the Israeli Supreme Court. The military are arguing for you know what, the *S-word* again, and the town is arguing for common sense and the chance to live in the same way as it has done for hundreds of years.

Hope is the only thing the activists, environmentalists and anyone who cares about democracy can hold onto when it comes to these towns, and the people who live in them. Their future is uncertain, and Israel's policy as an occupier has sought to rid them of their existence. And yet they fight, they persist despite years of being under occupation, with peace being wilfully avoided for political, financial, and religious gains.

So I ask you to put yourself on that rock, amongst your olive trees, with no water to give to your children or hope of a future. Your home has been demolished and yet a wall and many other homes, not available to you, are being built before you. You have nothing but the dust of their construction, carried on the breath of a cold autumn's wind, hindering the view to your past. You have nothing left. So please, tell me what will you do?

Waiting for Something to Come

27th October

Sitting amongst twenty people all eating their lunch in silence on the terrace. We're having a day of reflection before the retreat comes to its end tomorrow. I've actually, despite initial reservations, found the morning beneficial in helping to consolidate the retreat and the time we've shared. One activity I found really hard was standing before a partner and holding their gaze; it goes to show how little time we normally take to give people the full depth of our attention. It was uncomfortable to begin with, having to fight to put my sight back onto the sight of the person standing before me. We ended the morning session with a sharing – it was the first time since arriving in the Holy Land where I've been able to articulate my sentiments regarding the situation here clearly.

Before moving into the afternoon's activities, I will give a sense of place: the pockets of blue sky above are wrapped by thick white clouds, the wind is whispering in the leaves of the trees and the skull of an ox is facing me from the edge of the terrace. The switch from summer into autumn has taken place in just the last three days. The mornings and evenings now carry a chill and we even had a log fire burning this morning; I huddled close to its warmth reading Waiting For Godot. A Dutch gentleman has just stretched out beside me and one of the cats is heading this way. Anyway, I think it's time for the day's meditations to continue.

This day was powerful for many reasons. I think having ten Israelis arrive to reflect on the conflict with us made it all the more hard-hitting. I met people who had dedicated much of their lives to advocating peace, and in many cases had been ostracised from their own society for doing so. There was a look of gratitude and despair in their meeting with us; what had been the preoccupation of my month in Israel and Palestine had been a persistent factor throughout their lives. And fight as they have done, the suffering of living in Israel and in perpetual conflict is not going to go away any time soon. Not while the Israelis who we had the pleasure to share our time with are still a minority in the country, peace is still very low on the agenda of many Israelis, or they simply don't believe it can ever prevail.

It was a day of talking, a day of listening and in a sense a day of praying. Together, we sat in the spirit of peace and if enough people around the world can do this, really want this, then in the end peace will succeed because we can only continue to kill each other for so long until we meet a tipping point, the cold realisation that war, hatred, and greed have brought us nothing, and instead taken everything we hold dear away from us – life.

So before I come to the end of these reflections, and we're not quite there yet, I want to make a dedication and a thank you to all the Israelis that I met, along with all other Israelis that are fighting on the side of peace and democracy. I wish to dedicate this book to you. Without you and the work that you do, there is no hope of peace ever being attained. You are the shining light in a society that needs to be guided out of the darkness of fear it has been put into by political forces and an unwillingness to let the grave injustices of the past lie in the past. You are hope. And to the Israelis and internationals I spent time working with in Palestine, picking olives with the farmers and laughing together in the warm sunshine, I wish to thank you also. Every time I got pushed down by the occupation, felt that nothing could be done, I would see you and know then that all is not lost. Again, you are hope.

Following our day of reflection, it was time for us to depart and go our separate ways. The Being Peace retreat was over. But before leaving our hillside, the group came together in the tent and we had one final sharing – it is a moment that will never leave me. I was touched by everyone's honesty and felt strengthened by the bond we had formed.

When it came to my turn to speak, I felt compelled to share some lines I had read earlier that morning while sitting beside the fire with the early dawn sneaking into a sun-kissed sky. I lifted my notebook from my lap and opened it to where I had scribbled down a passage from Samuel Beckett's, *Waiting For Godot*. I poorly explained to the group that something in these lines resonated with me and my time spent with them.

In the play, the two main characters, Estragon and Valdimir, return each day to the same spot by a tree to meet with someone called Godot, but Godot has yet to arrive. At the time I couldn't pin-point what it was about this tale that I felt echoed my experience of being in Palestine and Israel. But now, I think I do. It's the struggle. Waiting for something you're sure will come, but have no date of when that will be, nor any idea of how it might present itself. And yet, still you wait and still you hold onto a tender hope that this thing, whatever it might be, peace perhaps, will come. Despite this uncertainty, we continue to write, we campaign further, we speak out louder, we stand before diggers, we try to reason with each other, to be rational, and to end it all we implore and we implore. We do all we can to change those things that are wrong. There might be a wall between us, but there are only good reasons to knock it down and weak excuses to let it stand.

Only Beckett knows if Godot eventually turns up, and if so what that may mean. But in the case of Israel and Palestine, Godot is peace and waiting is no longer an option, for this is not a play – it's real life. The truth of the situation is that we're not the ones waiting for peace, but peace is longingly waiting for us.

See You Now

30th October

The ping pat of the matkot players hitting a little ball to each other with their wooden rackets is ringing out over the call of the sea, a mild breeze is rippling the lace of my notebook's page mark and the sun is succumbing to the weight of the day and falling into the horizon before me. The white rocks beneath my feet are smooth with discarded pumpkin shells and sand scattered over them. Tel Aviv is certainly a "different world" to Jerusalem. It's highly secular, liberal and extremely busy (but Jerusalem wasn't exactly tranquil). So once the sun has been extinguished fully in the sea, I will head to a bar and begin to prepare myself for the writing to come.

People call Tel Aviv "The Bubble" and I had been eager to see why this was. I was equally eager to soak in all the treats that Tel Aviv had to offer: bars with a variety of beers, coffee shops, hummus restaurants and the end of a Mediterranean summer before departing for an English winter. I was also looking forward simply to walking around the city, to people-watch and to find out what makes Tel Aviv the bubble of the land. At the same time I wanted to learn what the occupation meant to people living here. How does it touch them? How does it compare with the occupation that I had seen and felt in the West Bank? So next morning I dashed out of my hostel early in search of my answers along with my first-needed treat.

31st October

Sitting in a small coffee shop somewhere in the Carmel Market, famous in Tel Aviv for its fresh produce and cheap prices. However, the owner of this place is nowhere to be seen (no, tell a lie, he's just arrived and now promptly grinding coffee beans). The stall holders outside are just unlocking the metal chests that hold their wares, looks mostly like jeans and silk shirts from here. After walking around last night in search of a beer, I finally found a bar off Allenby Street and spent the time plotting some stories. Afterwards, I headed back to the hostel and met with my roommates, they were from France and one of them was here because Jesus had told him to be. We then went to the rooftop and shared a shisha pipe. It's incredibly smooth to smoke but even so, after a few puffs I could feel my throat beginning to tire. The night was clear, allowing us to admire the first day of a waning moon. The rumble of helicopters scarred the silence *and soon I headed to bed. And now here I am, sitting in a little coffee shop and writing my way to the present — that of a slow-rising Tel Aviv. I'm also guessing that I will be able to go the whole day without even hearing the occupation mentioned once. It doesn't exist here!*

I should perhaps amend this. The occupation does exist in Tel Aviv, or the conflict does, but it's very different to the reality of the situation in Gaza and the West Bank. Writing this today, we have all seen images of the bus that was blown up in Tel Aviv in early November, or the rockets that were fired at Tel Aviv from Gaza during Operation Pillar of Defense. This is the occupation that Tel Aviv knows about, of occasionally being under attack. It does not see the life of the Palestinians in the West Bank or Gaza, and it will be offered little in the way of insight into this. It perhaps doesn't even know the full scale of the actions its government and military take in these territories, and this is why, I fear, the majority of people living in this wonderful city do not act or speak out against the injustices that its nation is engaged in.

The people of Tel Aviv are affected by the conflict, but they do not suffer from it enough to make the search for peace a priority. People simply want to live their lives, and this is fully understandable, but there comes a point, a point which should have come a long time ago, when people have to act before the situation becomes so big that even the bubble is at risk of bursting.

After savouring my coffee, I began to walk and I didn't stop until many hours later. Full of hummus and tired from seeing so many new sights, I left the promenade and walked along the sand, finally coming to sit by the shore.

Resting on the beach with children running into the sea before me, it's a little cloudy but still pleasing enough to bathe under this early autumn sun. I was able to find the hummus restaurant that I was recommended in the old city of Jaffa, about a thirty-minute walk along the seafront to reach. The hummus was great and served with half a raw onion and a stack of pita bread. Following this I ambled around the flea market for a bit and then sat myself here, on the sand, allowing my thoughts to drift this way and that with the breaking waves. The beach is by no means busy, but there are still lots of people enjoying the afternoon. I've no real plans or want to go anywhere; quite content to rest here and make the most of this warmth, by the close of tomorrow it will have *ended for me.*

But by the end of that day something I found deeply moving was to occur. I continued walking after sojourning on the beach and for long enough to find myself walking into nightfall and to a bench at the end of the Carmel Market, where it joins with Allenby Street. There I sat, watching the rivers of people passing by and also a bearded gentleman handing out little cards to everyone. He was a practising Jew, a rabbi I suspected, and beside him there was a table laden with extracts from the Torah, *kippahs*, and *tefillin* (prayer boxes). I continued observing him, intrigued by the curious contrast found in the location of this mobile prayer table and the whirlwind of busyness that comes with being in central Tel Aviv.

Occasionally people would come to stand before the table, predominantly young men and begin to dress themselves with the *tefillin*, one around the left arm and one on the forehead, and then crowning the head with a *kippah*. They would then close their eyes, focusing their concentration before reciting a passage from the Torah held open before them. I observed this moment of stillness and for the first time I felt a connection to what it meant to be Jewish. The man from Illinois who had told me back when my journey to the Holy Land first commenced that I "could never understand Judaism" was not entirely right. I was starting to understand it, to see the living dimension of this faith.

Later on, and toasting the completion of my trip with a beer in Port Said, a bar I had come to like near Allenby Street, I wrote about this experience and tried to understand what attracted me to it:

I was sitting very close and something struck me deeply as I watched the Jewish people stepping out of the middle of chaos to connect with their scripture. I began to observe all the people lost to the distractions of the consuming world around me, and decided I'd rather be standing at that table, touching upon a moment of contemplation, of truth seeking.

I wrote this soon after encountering the experience and I still stick to my words, be it with a measure of doubt. I will reservedly write in favour of many of the world's religions as they hold a great deal of humanity's treasure, and draw on us to consider how we can live in harmony with ourselves – but not always has this been reflected in how we live with each other. Religion has, through blind faith and divine/worldly ambition, unhelpfully constructed more walls between us and sought to hinder us from walking down a path we can all share.

These reflections are written to show that peace between Palestine and Israel is a dream that can be lived out. So all I hope is that, to begin with, Palestinians and Israelis can face each other, look into each other's eyes, holding the stare of the stranger they have previously been too afraid to meet and speak to them. To tell them simply, "I see you now."

1st November

Perched on a bar stool in Geneva airport, I scratched together the last of my shekels to convert into enough money to buy this tiny beer, but it nevertheless tastes sweet. My time in the Holy Land is over, and now it's down to my pen to bring these memories I hold onto alive once again. This journey ends for now, but does it really end? Isn't every day just another journey in its own way? Yes, it's merely the end of the beginning...

The Holy Land Is Somewhere in the Distance

February 2014 – another olive harvest has come and gone

Fourteen months have passed since my visit to the Holy Land. I think about it sometimes: my time there, the people I met and the words I saw. My experiences were woven into this book, into sentences and into stories. It was a book I had to write. It was all I could do in attempting to understand an occupation that is bleak and despairing. Still, what good will come of it?

During the European summer following my trip, spending my days folding linen and savouring life in the fertile and tranquil surroundings of Cubjac, a village in the Aquitaine region in south west France, and a place that, for the most part, time and modernity has let be; I picked out an ageing and well-read book amongst many other forgotten books on a shelf in a library. The cover was blue and captured a silver-haired woman walking along the side of an American highway, her smile deepening her wrinkles. Sown onto her jumper were the words 'Peace Pilgrim'.[6] I took this book away and read it on a grassy bank beside the river Auvézère, which feeds the surrounding countryside and corn fields. I have read it three times since.

This woman, who many have come to regard as a saint, spent most of her adult life walking across America relaying a very simple message: "This is the way of peace, overcome evil with good and falsehood with truth and hatred with love." Peace Pilgrim was able to complete her first pilgrimage, 25,000 miles, fuelled by her commitment to peace and love. She continued walking until her death, never losing faith in her message or the people she encountered along the way. Inspired by this humble and wonderful old woman, I wrote a sentence in my notebook while the low river rippled over the smooth stones below. I feel these words are the spine that binds my notes from the Holy Land together: *Awareness is the precursor to awakening.*

Of course, there is no reason why these words, this book, should make the slightest difference on the ground. After all, we've seen images of bulldozers smashing white concrete houses into rubble, we've seen images of the chaos caused after white phosphorus shells were dropped on Gaza during Operation Cast Lead, and we've seen images of buses being blown up in both Jerusalem and Tel Aviv. We've not woken up to the situation after being all too aware of what's happening, so why should this little book compel us to act now? It probably won't.

This book was written as much for me to exorcise the suffering I had witnessed along with the strong emotions stirred in me after having spent time in the realm of helplessness. This book was all I could do for the little boy who had compelled me to write it in the first place, the olive farmer's son from the ancient stone village of Deir Istiya. "You give me the life in Palestine," he had said, looking into my eyes and making me shiver despite the high heat while working under the Middle Eastern sun. "Talk the world," the boy commanded of me.

So this book of reflections was written with that little boy and his family never far from my heart and mind. I wrote, perhaps naively, that I did not want to cast judgement about right and wrong. I said the situation goes beyond this. Yet after reading back over my words, I am the first to admit that the sentiment of the book lays, not so much blame, but responsibility on Israel for peace not being achieved. It is not as simple as this, but in another sense it is. As an occupying force, Israel has continued to claim increasingly more land from the West Bank, achieved through strategically placed settlements and walls that encroach far beyond the Green Line, making any negotiations hard and perhaps meaningless.

Where will the hundreds of thousands of Israelis presently living in the West Bank go if peace is ever discovered?

I see this method of land theft as a slow process of strangulation. In twenty years, if an international body, the UN would make sense, does not actively step in to prevent the further encroachment into the West Bank, then what will be left to the Palestinians? Not much. The situation is bleak. The situation is despairing. However, and in the words of an Israeli activist I have been in communication with of late, "There is no reason to give up, things can change unexpectedly."

So I all too often find my mind wandering off to the Middle East. What's happening now? How did the olive harvest pass last autumn? It seems distant, a world away from my life living on a boat on a murky canal in the Georgian city of Bath. As I write this the birds are riotous with song outside and, what feels like a gift from above, the rain has stopped.

Occasionally a story will reach me from the Holy Land: *Netanyahu dismisses Kerry warning about price of failure in peace talks, Gaza's fragile ceasefire threatened by border clashes as Hamas weakens, Actor quits her role with charity after appearing as the glamorous face for an Israeli soda company that operates in the West Bank,* or *Israel approves 558 new homes in occupied*

East Jerusalem. Stories such as these are plenty, but the story we've been waiting for, the story that should have been captured and celebrated many years ago, the narrative of peace, is still to come. This story I cannot share with you now.

Unfortunately, I must share with you another incident, another injustice, which popped up in my inbox one Sunday morning at the end of January 2014. It tells the tale of Palestinian trees which have been uprooted in a small oasis in the middle of an unholy mess, a place where Israeli settlers have laid claim over Palestinian land. This area is called Wadi Kana. The message came from SanghaSeva, the organisation I worked with during my trip to the Middle East. They were in need of support to buy more olive trees to plant back into the ground where hundreds of others had been ripped out. The message concluded: *This small, and perhaps futile act, is all we can do. But is it small, is it futile? When Gandhi undertook the salt march, when Martin Luther King took to the streets, these were futile undertakings. Replanting trees is civil disobedience; (it) is an act of not accepting an authority you didn't vote for, it is rejecting an authority that doesn't care for your rights.*

I looked up from the words on the screen and out of the boat's window, watching the winter sunshine dance over the canal, before looking out across the valley where I was moored with the typical Bath limestone houses dressing its slopes. I looked into the patchy blue sky and towards the horizon, trying to picture the valley that is home to Wadi Kana. "Yes," I whispered, "the Holy land is somewhere in the distance."

Wadi Kana, The West Bank
A fictional story, mostly.

The farmer sits; he waits and he watches over the valley. The rocky soil crumbles into red dust between the hardened skin over his fingers. He grinds it further, watching and waiting.

The man had stirred from his dwelling in darkness. His family lay on the threadbare rugs on the floor around him, the softness of their dreams helping to relieve the hardness of the stone on which they slept. It's early, the farmer had arrived as the winter sun was just peaking over the hilltops. Dewdrops clung to the little leaves on his trees, olives are yet to dot their branches, with the harvest too far away for the farmer to think much of it. But still, the harvest is why he sits and watches. He looks out across the rolling green and brown hills, with white craggy rocks and boulders speckling their ancient slopes. In spring, the red petals of the wildflowers dance all around in the warming breeze. The farmer loves those flowers, he thanks them for returning each year, they help to remind him that life is beautiful. He forgets this sometimes. He doesn't want to, but he does.

He gazes upwards. Amidst the blossoming light of a new day the invaders' white houses can be seen crowning the hilltops. The farmer's home used to be located in the valley too, he tells the children this every day. They must remember. He gave them the metal key that once opened the door to the house he had loved. Now he must live in the dusty town of Deir Istiya. It is lovely in its own way, but it is not Wadi Kana. Besides, he was not granted permission to build a home there, in his own land he was denied by the court of another. The farmer cannot respect or adhere to what the invaders say he can and cannot do, he has children, they need a home, so he has built his house and he will rebuild it when they come and bull-doze it to the ground. He will rebuild it time and time again. He has to, he has children. What's more, he did not give them permission to destroy his first home, he had papers of ownership over the house and land, but they destroyed it all the same.

The landscape is changing so quickly now that he fears he will forget where his home once stood. *The children will remember*, he thinks rubbing his temples with his dirty fingers. His head pains him. His wife tells him it's stress. He tells her it's occupation. The invaders are going to make a town here, the farmer knows it. The settlements have strategically circled the valley, ready to mould into one settlement, across the entirety of the West Bank expansion and strangulation exist as one. His olive trees are trapped in the heart of the invaders' presence. He kicks a stone by his foot, sending it tumbling down the slope, towards the spring pool that is visible in the basin below. The water was pure and plentiful before they arrived, plentiful enough for his father to grow citrus fruits and grain. The land was rich with life, now it is rich with their tourists and young invaders riding through it on quad bikes, and this is how they treat and define a nature reserve. They polluted it first, drained it of its water to quench their settlements' thirst and now they say it's special, and the farmer is spoiling it through his presence and with his trees. He shakes his head. It hurts.

As a little boy he would play in the spring; it was a haven in the summer months, when the surrounding land would bake and crack under the high Middle Eastern sun. He recalls jumping and playing in the water with his friends. Not many of his childhood friends are with him now, they left when their lands were robbed, distraught and desperate. How many have died of a broken heart? The farmer waits for his own heart to do the same. At night, in darkness and silence, he lies awake and waits for his heart to shatter and death to release him from the ailments of life. In his paradise he pictures only Wadi Kana, as he had seen it as a boy with sunbeams dancing on the surface of the water and the wildflowers pretty as when he had first seen his wife picking olives on her family's grove. Their first embrace had been in Wadi Kana. Out of sight of observing orthodox eyes, he sweetly kissed her. *Yes,* the farmer thinks, *I once touched life.* His dry lips curve into a subtle smile. It's easier sometimes, to spend your days living in memory, choosing to stay a small carefree boy, splashing around in water, not wanting to be the helpless old man he has become, sitting on a cold rock in winter. He sits. He waits. He watches.

The last harvest was not easy. He gets cross with himself when he thinks this, for no harvest is ever easy. Still, it was hard on his aging body, the days were long, and the reward just enough to compel him to do it again this year. What choice does he have? There is nothing else. He has olive trees and a home constantly under threat of demolition. Without the trees, the farmer knows he will have nothing. *That's what they want*, he says to the diminished spring below. There is a plan; he is not blind to it. No-one really is. The invaders claiming the hilltops know it. They plan to leave the farmer with nothing. He cannot build. He cannot move or leave. He cannot comfort his children with a few whispers of a better future. He cannot lie. He cannot survive. But that's the plan, isn't it?

The farmer looks up from his thoughts, questioning how the children had confronted the invaders when they had last driven their armoured trucks and flashed their guns around the village square; this being their way of letting the Palestinians know that they have the power, while the Palestinians have none. Still, the farmer thought the children's response was too strong, that they shouldn't be singing such songs: *"5-6-7-8: Israel - is a - fascist - state."* It will not help them towards a shared future. But then, sometimes the farmer finds himself singing it with them. He did so when their authorities came to mark his trees, it was the only resistance he had, a children's song: *"5-6-7-8: Israel - is a - fascist - state."* He told them they had marked too many, that the trees were older than the invading parks authority declared them to be. They left but not without leaving their mark. The farmer slowly and pensively walked amongst his grove, surveying each and every blood red spot painted onto the trunks of his beloved trees, the only source of livelihood his family could depend on. His olives were the one remaining purpose he could reason to be alive at all. *If it was not for the children*, this thought has plagued him more and more in the years since his trees were first identified for uprooting.

The invaders say they are a threat to the natural beauty of the reserve; the farmer was born a Palestinian, so therefore he was born a threat and nothing he could have done in life would have made any difference. He grows olive trees in the soils that he owns, but still, this is threatening. The invaders have lowered the water table, disfigured the landscape and polluted the streams, but their actions, strangely, are in order with the balance of a nature reserve's harmony. But of course, we are in Palestine, so it would be pointless to bring up a silly ideology such as democracy, ideologies have already brought too much hurt and immorality to this one piece of land.

After the trees had been branded and targeted for destruction, the farmer walked home to Deir Istiya, the call to prayer resounded over the village with only a scattering of donkeys and goats, bells jingling at their necks, to be seen on the narrow and solemn streets. He had to tell his family. It stirred a constricting pain in his chest to see the puzzled expression on his children's little faces, their wide eyes weeping with fear and unknowing. So the farmer's vigil of waiting commenced; every morning he rose before dawn to come to this vantage point looking out across the valley, overlooking his trees that shivered in the morning breeze below. He willed something to change. He willed them not to come. But all the farmer can really do is sit, and watch, and wait.

The call of a bird sounds overhead, he observes the eagle gliding on the thermals as it effortlessly moves across the blank blue sky. Flight and freedom, two things the farmer may never know. The bird becomes a speck on the horizon as it continues stalking the prey unknowingly going about its life below. An attack, the end of existence, can swoop down and blanket it in darkness at any moment. The bird suddenly drops from the sky, wings pointed back as it becomes a bullet, the arrow of its beak targeting its helpless victim. Yes, something is about to die. The farmer follows its descent with his vision quickly settling on the cloud of dust swelling and swirling upwards, tracing the valley basin. He hears engines. He hears the thud of his heart. He is alone. They are coming. They are coming.

He stands from his rock, beginning to make his way down the jagged slope, stumbling at its base as he begins hobbling and running along the broken road, which the invaders would not let the farmers repair. He gulps for air as he heads towards his grove. Their Jeeps are stationed across the road, blocking his path. Soldiers stand before him, guns cradled in their arms, the metal glimmering in the sunshine. The farmer shouts at them, the soldiers step forward and raise their guns. The farmer runs to a stop and looks into their eyes. *You have not the right to be here*, he tells them pitifully. The soldiers respond with silence. The morning is then filled by the heavy drone of diggers. Beyond the Jeeps, the famer knows there is a crime being perpetrated. He screams. The soldiers stand unmoved, their expressions trained and hearts hardened; some appear as though just out of college, maybe a few of them have resisted a life of conditioning, and can still see this man before them, still appreciate his pain and suffering, or perhaps not, for they do not move. The soldiers force him back. The grinding of the diggers' steel tracks releases the farmer's pleas as he drops to his knees. The soldiers do nothing but watch and wait.

There is a splintering sound of roots being ripped out from the soil of this land bizarrely defined as holy; the way nature laces a row of blushing olives to the branches of the farmer's trees is holy; the passing of the seasons, the wildflowers in spring, these are holy. No, there is not much left to be found here now which is worthy of being defined as holy. No-one is foolish enough to believe that holiness could be truly maintained out of evil, but then again – some must. The diggers whine as they smash into the ground, scooping the soil and trees up with their bulging buckets. The farmer weeps on his knees, his tears trickling down his dry wrinkled face. *Please*, he says to the soldiers standing over him. They say nothing.

It did not take them long to undo nature's work; she has given years of sunshine to the trees, and the farmer had given years of nurture. No, it did not take long for this to be undone. The diggers move with intent around the grove, the trees they rip up are taken away, not left as evidence to show what has taken place here. The farmer knows what they have done, the number of trees that were illegally removed; but he is Palestinian so his voice is worthless. Who will listen? What could be done? The diggers go on their way, their work completed. The trucks carrying his uprooted livelihood go with them, and the soldiers then turn on their boots and get into their Jeeps. The vehicles drive back out of the valley, until there is only the farmer, with the renewed silence stained only by his whimpering pleas. He struggles to his feet.

With his hands held to his head, the farmer walks around his grove, holes now rest where his trees once stood. He walks over the tracks left by the diggers before coming to stand over one hole in the ground. It is a fitting grave, the farmer would lie in it but it is not long enough. He will die soon; his heart will break tonight, after he is forced to tell his family. The echo of nothing ripples around the grove. The man stands in the middle of it. He has nothing left to watch. He has nothing left to wait for. He has just that, nothing. He stands in the middle of the grove, not knowing where to go or what to do.

The sun rests over the hilltops and the settlements that have taken rule over the farmer's existence. *How has this come to pass?* He lowers his hands from his head and looks down into the ruptured ground, shadows pool in the hole with threads of severed roots still woven through the soil. The farmer closes his eyes, recalling the joy he had once known here, before his eyes open to see the destitution it has been turned into. Teardrops swell and fall like rain to the broken earth beneath him, salty and invisible to the world and reason. He turns and climbs down into the hole, where he then sits cradling his knees to his chest. The farmer will die in Wadi Kana; he will die with the memory of being a boy and laughing as he swims in the spring. And so it has come to this, truth now only to be found in memory. The farmer sits in the hole and amongst the shadows, remembering and waiting.

How Do You Make Right That Which Is Wrong?

Interview with a spokesperson from Engaged Dharma, an organisation that has been following the situation at Wadi Kana since 2012.

It's Saturday February 15th 2014. It's windy and the boat is creaking on its ropes as it's pushed against the bank. It's 6pm in Bath, 8pm in Jerusalem. Dusk has already been overcome by night and I'm huddled next to the wood burner and before my laptop, attentively waiting for my contact in Israel to appear online. *Shabbat would have just come to its end,* I think, imagining the streets and shops that fill the western part of the Holy City to be opening after a period of prayer, contemplation and religious obligation. I check the time again, flicking between my emails and the questions I have prepared.

I had arranged an interview with a spokesperson from Engaged Dharma, friends of SanghaSeva, and another organisation that is working hard for peace. I've come to know that dharma can carry many definitions, and not one word in the western language can claim to directly define it. I think of it simply as spirituality, equally a term which does not hold a universal definition. When I meditate on it more deeply then I understand it as the way of being; how we approach and interact with this fleeting gift of life.

I had already met my contact from Engaged Dharma. He had kindly shown and talked us around the cruel and bizarre happenings at al-Walaja, a Palestinian village that had been fully enclosed by the separation barrier. He was a stoic young man, an Israeli who had formed many friendships with the Palestinians who he campaigns tirelessly with in the pursuit of justice. "I don't feel I am "helping" Palestinians," he conveyed to me, "I am working and struggling in solidarity with them." It was a striking image: watching the villagers of al-Walaja clasping the hand of this Israeli. They were grateful. They walked side by side, surveying the diminishing landscape together and discussing the next viable action to take. "Sometimes we (Engaged Dharma) initiate, sometimes our Palestinian partners lead – the best is when we do it jointly," he explained. "Likewise I think my acquaintances in Walaja see me as a friend and as a comrade – not as a saviour."

Engaged Dharma has been working with the farmers from Wadi Kana since the Israel Nature and Parks Authority (INPA) first issued, in April 2012, uprooting orders for 1,400 olive trees. These are, to be clear, orders to uproot Palestinian trees on Palestinian land. In response to this the villagers, with the help of a lawyer appointed by the Palestinian Authority (PA), attempted to oppose the orders on legal grounds. The bizarre nature of a diplomacy in the Holy Land means this is passed through the Israeli Supreme Court which, as is the case with settlements, can decide what is to be built and destroyed in the West Bank. The court ruled that trees planted after 2010 were to be removed. But the parks authority marked far more than this, 2,100 trees in all. The farmers could do nothing but make another legal appeal, resulting in the parks authority being told to remark the trees. They did so. Members from Engaged Dharma were present this time. They told the rangers that they were marking trees older than two years. They told them that they were acting against the court ruling.

In January 2014, after launching a campaign, Engaged Dharma sent a letter with 565 signatures to the Israeli Minister of the Environment. A meeting was arranged between Engaged Dharma and the Israeli Civil Administration to survey the trees marked for uprooting. The meeting did not inspire much hope but a second was arranged for January 29th. This meeting did not come to pass. On January 23rd 2014, the Civil Administration arrived in Wadi Kana at daybreak, escorted by the army and uprooted hundreds of trees, the farmers claimed 1,000. No evidence was left; trees which could be proven to be older than two years, trees that might be incriminating, were taken away. Engaged Dharma were called and told the news; they immediately made their way to the wadi. What happens now? How do you make right that which is wrong? I hope to find out.

A circle goes green on my laptop screen, the word *online* pops up; two hours have passed since first sitting down to make a connection to the Middle East. It will be getting late there. I press call. After a few echolike *Hellos*, the interview with Engaged Dharma follows:

M. Small: *How can an Israeli parks authority declare Wadi Kana to be a nature reserve in the first place? Being that it is in the West Bank, does the land not fall under the control of the Palestinian Authority (PA)?*
Engaged Dharma: It was declared in 1983, so that's before Oslo and before there was a PA. It was done at a time when the whole of the West Bank was under military rule, and the actual mechanism of declaration was through the army. The army is the authority governing the West Bank and there's no legislative body, so there's this procedure

where the army issues a regulation, and then the area is declared a park or a nature reserve. And once it's declared a nature reserve then it comes under the authority of the Israel Nature and Parks Authority. Today, Wadi Kana is, like 60 percent of the West Bank, in area C which by the Oslo agreement is under full Israeli control with no authority for the PA.

M.S: *Can you describe the scene at Wadi Kana after arriving on the morning following the uprooting of the trees?*
E.D: Because we do not live close, we had to drive and by the time we had got there it was exactly as the army was leaving. From what the people told us, they [the army] were there for like two to three hours. Soldiers wouldn't let Palestinians come close to the area where the uprooting took place, there was some tear gas and so on.

When we came and the army was going out, all of us, there were a few dozen Palestinians, […] went inside. At a certain point we could still smell the tear gas, and there were maybe six or seven military cars, like Jeeps and so on, coming out the opposite way. When we arrived in the area you couldn't really see much because the trees that were uprooted were, I guess, put on trucks which left through another way, not the way we were coming from. So by the time we were allowed to enter, there was not much to be seen except for the land which we know very well with several hundred trees on it, which were not there. The people [Palestinians] themselves, of course, were very…what can you say? They were upset. They were angry. They were relatively calm but it was clear that they were very upset at this.

M.S: *What can the farmers and you do now?*
E.D: We estimate that about half the trees marked for uprooting were uprooted. So there is still the other half to prevent uprooting, for this you either have demonstrations or you try a legal way. Deir Istiya people, a year and a half ago, were demonstrating against the uprooting, but now they're not doing this. I'm not sure what changed for them, but they are not, so there's left the legal avenue which they have already taken. The [Israeli] Supreme Court gave a decision saying trees that were planted after April 2010 were the trees to be uprooted. It seems, as far as we can tell, that the trees have been planted before April 2010, so we need to be able to prove it and to prevent the rest of the trees from being uprooted. We've been trying to do it, but it's a very peculiar situation because the people who have the authority to uproot the trees and will decide whether to accept our proof or not are the army and the parks authority which decided on the uprooting in

the first place. When we try and meet with them they don't necessarily want to meet with us, so it's not so simple. We're acting as if we're in a normal situation where if you have a grievance you go with your claim to the relevant authority and they are obliged to hear you out and regard you seriously. But this is occupation in which the authorities [i.e. Israeli occupation authorities] don't have sympathy for the [Palestinian] population and its supporters, and in the first place their "responsibility" is to promote Israeli interests and not to serve the Palestinian population.

When we meet with them, they say, what we're [INPA] doing is perfectly legitimate, if you think we're not going according to the court ruling then appeal to the court. But the court has already given its decision; the judges don't go and start measuring trees, and decide how old they are. It's a very annoying situation where they're trying to get rid of us and we're not really sure where to put pressure on. So far we've managed to get a meeting and we've been promised another meeting with the legal advisor of the army. Hopefully until that meeting happens nothing will change and we're confident that we can prove the trees have been planted earlier, because we have aerial photos from before 2010 where the trees can be seen. Hopefully we will manage to do it. In a very optimistic case we will be able to convince them that the trees that were uprooted were also planted earlier, and then someone will have to explain why they violated the court's decision. We're not sure we'll be able to [because] we have to convince the body that wants to uproot the trees, so it's not an easy thing to do.

M.S: *And they've also taken the uprooted trees, leaving no evidence.*
E.D: Exactly. And then there's the long-term thing which is one of the most important consequences; the area, although it is owned by Palestinians, it's not so close to Deir Istiya. It's a few kilometres away from Deir Istiya and it's surrounded by four or five settlements. It's a valley, or a wadi, so they are above the wadi. The councils of the settlements have this plan of having this area for their use as a nature and resort area. They've recently drafted a plan for an eight million shekel budget for developing the area for tourism. It looks like there will be a constant pushing out of the Palestinian farmers and maybe Palestinians who also go there just to enjoy the place. So in all kinds of ways, they will be pushed out or their presence there limited. This is something we have to find ways to work against. That's something we need to think over. With regards to exposing these plans and trying to block them, this is something that

is maybe in our [Engaged Dharma] hands, but the right way to do it is to strengthen the Palestinian presence in the wadi, and this of course depends greatly on the people of Deir Istiya; how much energy they have for it; how much priority they give to it. If they decide they are going to do it then we will support.

M.S: *How does the situation taking place in Wadi Kana fit into the occupation as a whole? What does it say about Israel as an occupying force?*

E.D: You have the general patterns. For whatever reason, that doesn't even need to be thought in advance, but for whatever reason in that area [Wadi Kana], there are quite a few settlements. We're speaking about a piece of land; it's a big piece of land, several hundred dunams [approximately 170 acres]. It's between Israeli settlements and Palestinian villagers, and it's owned by Palestinians. There is a constant effort by the Israelis to seize more. You can say there is a constant effort by the Palestinians to keep it, okay, but they are keeping land that's not only nationally theirs but also in terms of property rights. This we know from the whole West Bank; sometimes it's private initiatives of settlers, many times it's plans initiated by the government. Here [in Wadi Kana] we have many signs that it's initiated by the councils of the settlements. The councils are a formal body, they are a part of the State of Israel or the Israeli establishment. I don't know, you make the judgement, what it says about Israel as an occupier, but this is the picture. It's not something, for me as an Israeli, it's not something I'm proud of.

The fact is that sometimes Israelis that are maybe not extremist, but they support settlements, they try to say something like, look there's Palestinians living here, there's Israelis living here, and we need to find a way to live in harmony together. Again as an Israeli I'm not happy to say it; we have a very long history of Israel using its power and its ability to plan and to strategise in order to fulfil what it sees as its interests, or at least its desires at the expense of Palestinians. So this suggestion of lets live together and put the conflict behind us, [or] if only both sides accepted each other then they could live in peace with each other, it's not so simple in my eyes. Specifically for that point, if you are supporting a two-state solution, and you are sympathetic to one of the Israeli claims saying, look we've been controlling the area for forty-five years, there's settlements, people are living there, you cannot just kick people out of their homes, if you see that there's some logic in it and you say, okay we will not go back to the '67 borders, but we will somehow take into account that the reality has changed and there's all sorts of consequences, in that case Wadi Kana is exactly the area where Israel wants the border to pass. That's assuming that the Israeli government is willing to have a Palestinian State, willing to get out of some of the West Bank. Then because of these four or five settlements [in Wadi Kana], it's about 17,000 Israelis in that area, and from that area back to the Green Line there's a few other settlements, so we're talking about a few tens of thousands of Israelis living in those settlements, then Wadi Kana is exactly where the border is to pass according to Israel. Israel will do as much as possible to keep that area and not as a part of the Palestinian State.

M.S: *Does this explain the reason why the wall is being planned to pass through Wadi Kana?*
E.D: Yes, many people, some of them, are not a part of the establishment, they are critical of the establishment, and some of them are part of the establishment and are just saying this is what we are doing; the separation barrier is supposed to outline the route of the border as Israel would like to see it. Just to clarify, most of the separation barrier has been built since 2002. I think massive construction ended about 2006, more or less. There were large parts that

weren't constructed and this [section passing through Wadi Kana] is one of them. [This] doesn't mean that, tomorrow, Israel cannot start constructing it, but right now the barrier is there on the map.

M.S: *Can you describe the concept behind Engaged Dharma? Why did you start the organisation and what were your aims?*
E.D: There were a few of us, or maybe not so few, that were dharma practitioners and were also engaged in peace activities or solidarity activities over the years. A few of us felt in 2009 that things were getting very very bad. It was after the war in Gaza and around the times of the elections of the previous Netanyahu government, when the elections themselves were very... There was a lot of aggressive propaganda against Palestinians as a part of those elections.

Around that time, a few of us got together and said okay we're doing what we're doing as people with activist groups, but the dharma community which we belong to can contribute a lot to promoting peace, to engaging productively with the conflict. We feel that on the one hand, dharma practitioners and dharma communities are obliged to take the situation of occupation into consideration, and to relate to it and to act with regards to it because we see the values of our practice as being relevant to it. That's on the one hand, on the other hand, we feel that our *sangha* [spiritual community] does have a lot to contribute, not that it should, but it also has many good things to offer. That's our aim.

The *sangha*, I don't know how it is in Europe, but in Israel, the *sangha* shies away from political issues and prefers not to bring them in. So our main issue is that we are like a bridge between the people in the *sangha* and the reality of the occupation. So we make opportunities for people to come into places like Deir Istiya, like Wadi Kana, to see for themselves, to see Palestinians, to understand the conditions of life under military rule. We frame it in the context of dharma, the things dharma speaks of and the values that dharma nurtures. We use the practice in order to give us support. It can be a shaking experience when you realise that maybe your side, your country, what you identify with, is really disrupting peoples' lives, and has a lot of responsibility for a lot of violence that is happening. It's not such an easy transformation to take place, or even if it does take place, then how do you go back to your society and what do you feel regarding your society which keeps on supporting this violence? So we use the practice of awareness, meditation, listening, the commitment to non-violence, and the awareness of inter-connectedness. Many things that give us support as activists, and support the people that, through us, come and touch with this reality.

M.S: *With respect to helping me to envisage the scene in Wadi Kana, how were the trees marked for uprooting?*
E.D: We were there one of the times that the parks authority inspector came to mark the trees. They go with this spray bottle and they go along the trees and they just spray a colour on the trunk. That's a mark that the tree is to be uprooted. Like I told you, they claim that they marked trees that were planted after April 2010, and they say, we brought an expert that checked the trees and told us which trees to mark, but we were there and we saw that there was no expert. Their boss was just pointing in one direction and saying, *Here, you mark 200 trees.* And then he was pointing in another direction, saying, *Here, you mark eighty trees.*

M.S: *And what colour was the paint?*
E.D: They came in July to mark. They marked in red. They marked 2,000 trees, a much bigger number than the original number they said in the warrants, and again trees that were old. The lawyer of the farmers sent a letter of complaint. So they came again in November, that's the time we were there, and then they marked in blue.

M.S: *In our previous communication, you mentioned "zero-sum game" as the way in which politicians are approaching the overall situation. Do you mean all or nothing by this?*

E.D: It means that my gain is your loss and your gain is my loss. In the issue of land, it makes perfect sense; Wadi Kana will either be Palestinian or Israeli. It can't be both. The prevailing attitude in Israeli politics is that the negotiations, the way they are done now, require no atmosphere of reconciliation. There's no recognising of the legitimate needs of Palestinians. There are no declarations that try to promote some sort of understanding, recognition and reconciliation. It's all about: we don't like them, we don't trust them, but we have no choice, and we should therefore try to do it in the way that we get as much as possible out of it, in all terms, not only in the term of land. There's this talk about the security needs of Israel, so no-one thinks that security can be achieved through reconciliation, or through trusting Palestinians. Security is only with Israeli tanks based on the Jordan River, which is supposed to be the Palestinian State.

*

I thank my contact for speaking with me and I wish him well with his endeavours. Nothing is certain as to what will happen next at

Wadi Kana. The Civil Administration could return at any time to uproot the remaining trees. The construction of the wall may recommence and scar this piece of land, which is almost hypocritically defined as a resort and nature reserve. The Palestinian farmers might lose everything that they had sincerely believed they owned, or, through the union with organisations like SanghaSeva and Engaged Dharma, they might be able to protect and hold onto that which is rightly and legally theirs. Nothing is certain. The story of injustice and power games at Wadi Kana continues…

The Wall Between Us

Last summer I gave a first draft of this book to a friend from Tel Aviv. I have him largely to thank for my persevering with it to publication. He told me that as he was reading it he thought, *I know this place.* He even picked out a line I had written *...guns and holiness go together in Jerusalem...* telling me that he happened to agree. Having this feedback from an Israeli, and an Israeli who had first helped to set me on a path to the Middle East, was wonderful. In fact, I would like to take a moment to tell you how I came to be interested in this conflict, for up until four years ago I knew very little about it.

Sometimes you find yourself, intentionally or not, stepping out of society. Normally it's for a short break, a holiday to a remote island, a weekend walking parts of the splendour of the Welsh coastline, or sometimes it can be for a prolonged period. My move away came with wanting to be a writer. I was the co-owner of an up-and-coming speciality coffee shop in Bath, but occasionally I felt this niggle of doubt that grew until I was left no choice but to leave my friends and partnership in the business to free myself enough to commit to learning the art and discipline of writing. Not having an income meant I was forced to be creative in what I did and where I went, thus I ended up volunteering in a meditation centre in France. My days were spent mixing red clay in plastic buckets before slapping it on the new walls of a straw bale house. The work was hard, the days beautifully hot and the opportunities to write plentiful. In this setting, a place where people arrived from all around the world, I met a secular Israeli who first gave me insight into the occupation and how the situation was knotted so tightly in complexity that no-one could foretell how it would turn out.

With my curiosity heightened I asked if he would answer some questions; I didn't know then that it was to be the first interview I was to facilitate as a writer. I came with a big wad of paper and we sat on a bench by the river, protected from the sun under the shade of an oak tree. We were there for three hours. He took me back to the fall of the Ottoman Empire, to the British mandate held over the State of Palestine at the start of the twentieth century, to the day of *Nakba* in 1948 when the State of Israel was declared and a Palestine for Palestinians potentially lost forever, and then he spoke of the bubbling excitement felt at the near peace that came with the work of Yitzhak Rabin, the then Israeli prime minister and recipient of the Nobel Prize, before this turned into absolute deflation after his assassination in 1995 by a right-wing Israeli who opposed

Rabin's work on the Oslo peace agreement.

It was a whirlwind of a history lesson and throughout it all I wanted to know more. I wanted to know who was to blame for peace not being attained. But my friend had to keep reinforcing the point to me, "It is not that simple." In the first place, he told me that the "Palestinians have to sort their shit out." He was referring to the obstinate view of groups like Hamas in Gaza, who refuse to recognise the State of Israel. Israel is a State and the more it feels under threat, the further away peace remains. Hamas, and groups like them, need to do the best thing for Palestinians and stop providing Israel with excuses not to be searching for and promoting peace. The interview continued with my friend telling me about another assassination, one that is so telling of how utterly tragic this conflict is.

There are refugee camps dotted across the West Bank. I have written about Dheisheh in Bethlehem and how it has grown into a network of breezeblock buildings and corrugated iron. These camps were initially set up for those Palestinians whose homes now lie raised to the ground or in ruin in the State of Israel. In the north of the West Bank there is a particularly impoverished camp, Jenin. Here, from the things I have read and the videos I have watched, life is hard; employment is scarce and some young men and women, after growing up feeling stripped of existence in the camp and hounded by Israeli power, have martyred themselves, killing Israeli civilians in the process. The camp, on first sight, has no future. The Palestinians who live in it have no ambitions they could ever foresee as achievable. But a glimmer of hope did come to this camp, it still stands there today, and it is called, The Freedom Theatre.

Not long before I interviewed my Israeli friend under an oak tree in a land distant from the West Bank, an assassination had been committed in the Jenin refugee camp. The then General Director of the theatre was shot dead by an unknown gunman. The deceased was a man named Juliano Mer Khamis. I wish to include a brief overview of his life and death because the story of the theatre, Jenin being a place I haven't even been to, is the story that locked my attention to the Israel and Palestine conflict.

What can be achieved through something so play-filled as art? I would argue an awful lot. Mer Khamis believed this, and his mother, Arna Mer Khamis, believed this also. She was an Israeli who came to the Jenin refugee camp with the vision of helping the children who were suffering from depression, post-traumatic stress and a lasting fear that comes from living under a military occupation. Arna opened The

Stone Theatre, giving the children the space to play and create and to release their fear and anger that might otherwise manifest in a multiplicity of psychological disorders.

Mer Khamis documented his mother's work in a film, *Arna's Children*. It captures the helplessness of Jenin, the empowerment Arna's method of utilising creativity brought to the children, and the destructive power Israel can muster when it sees fit, destroying The Stone Theatre in an invasion on the camp in 2002. One of the hardest-hitting moments in the film is when Mer Khamis returns to the camp years after first filming the children making theatre with his mother; Arna had since died of cancer, her theatre had been destroyed, and he records how two of the children, grown into men so angered by their incarceration in poverty and forced to suffer the deaths of loved ones and friends, had driven a truck into Israel where they began to open fire and kill innocent civilians. They were themselves shot dead. It is a harrowing watch and *Arna's Children* does not end with any falsity about hope in Jenin. There is none.

However, Mer Khamis, following his return to the camp to make the documentary, decided to reopen the theatre. This time he called it The Freedom Theatre. He was himself a volatile and controversial individual; he was half-Israeli and half-Palestinian and a potential outcast to both societies. He had had some success as an actor in Israel, but he decided to put his energy into Jenin and into the theatre. Watching the videos of him outlining his vision, you cannot fail to see the strength of his character and commitment to fighting the occupation through art: *"My dream is that The Freedom Theatre will be the major force, cooperating with others in generating a cultural resistance, carrying on its shoulders universal values of freedom and justice."*

The theatre was launched and work started on productions that would not only be a stand against occupation but also a stand against traditional customs that, if not confronted, had the effect of stifling creativity and liberty. The fact that Mer Khamais was not afraid to put on such shows as George Orwell's *1984*, or *Alice In Wonderland*, with girls being given the chance to perform in public, along with culturally taboo subjects finding their way into drama, made the theatre a target of more conservative members of the Jenin camp. Mer Khamais would not compromise his definition of freedom in all meanings of the word, and, sadly, it appears that this likely led to his death. His killer was never caught but the theatre describes the perpetrator as an "unknown enemy of culture and freedom."

If the killer was from the camp, as is

suspected, then it shows how sorry the situation is; a man who has tried to liberate its young through the modes and mediums of creative expression was killed because he also tackled tradition. The theatre still remains and there is a tour planned to the UK in 2015. It continues to provide the young of the camp with a means to tackle the occupation through cultural resistance. It is non-violent and I hope it inspires many other projects to fight in the same way. The theatre gives the children and young people of Jenin an opportunity to dream, to be something other than trapped and defenceless. If children can dream then what's to stop some of these dreams from being lived out, like the dream of peace, perhaps. The Freedom Theatre is a dream maker; it is a good thing in a region where so many bad things have happened. One day I hope to see a production.

*

Nearing the end of these reflections, a question remains: is there ever going to be peace between Israel and Palestine? After spending time between the two cultures, after thinking and searching for a simple answer as to why this wall between two people persists, I cannot pretend the situation is anything different than it is. Presently, peace will not be found. There is no lust for it politically and no strong incentives for it to be pursued to its attainment. Peace for peace's sake doesn't seem strong enough. It does not mean the dream of achieving peace is lost. The grounds simply need to be ploughed for the seeds of peace to be sown. The two warring neighbours, as best they can, have to move on from the injustices of the past. Peace is a compromise, but it is the best of compromises. It's about finding a common thread that unites us all. That thread is life.

Today, the Holy Land is a battleground of wants, needs and expectations. The religious settlers want it to return to the biblical land written about in scripture: the economic settlers might not have fully understood the neighbourhood they were moving into, but the subsidies they were offered were too good to turn down. The everyday settler just wants a roof over their head and a fenced off garden to potter about in, frankly bored and increasingly frustrated by the "Arab question". Then there are the Palestinians, the far-rights who refuse to ever accept a nation state for the Jews, the fishermen that look out to sea off the coast of Gaza, wondering how many trips they have left, and what pitiful catch they'll make in a teardrop of the ocean, restricted by Israel to a six-nautical-mile fishing zone. There are the labourers that make the dehumanising crossing from the West Bank into Israel every day, watched over by armed soldiers as they wait in long queues at checkpoints, beleaguered by turnstile after turnstile and finally there are the olive farmers I worked with in the groves, sipping sweet tea or eating another lunch of pita bread and hummus. Some want peace, others simply want to bring in their crop – peace is something politicians say to cameras, peace is a word too easily exploited.

But despite the walls in the way and the closed minds of many, peace is avidly being fought for. In my trip to the Holy Land, I met people from all around the world seeking to know what chance peace has. I worked with some in olive groves. I meditated with others on green nurtured hillsides, and I was moved time and time again to learn how many of these peace seekers were Israeli. Peace can happen.

As things play out on the ground, with the overcrowded prison that is the Gaza Strip, the lack of strong united leadership in the West Bank, the theft of more land by Israel and far-right politicians that have played on fear for too long; yes, I agree, peace looks like it has no chance. But I choose to put my conviction in people. It is our innate capacity to change, to survive, that has seen us spiral to newer and greater achievements, be that in technology or simply in our ability to meet the demands of living an existence that is always underwritten by uncertainty. Our species has committed horrors that are and will always remain beyond comprehension, but we have overcome these horrors. We have still to learn from them, we are still to arrive at a point in time where we know no hate, only love. Still, we are here, we are not perfect, life is not always easy, sometimes we have to get lost before we're found, and it is in this that hope is maintained – discovery.

Peace is a thing to be discovered. The most important thing that goes into making any discovery is that the quest for it is sincere. There is only one way I could think and would like to conclude this book of reflections, it is by saying a heartfelt, "Thank you." I wish to thank every peace seeker that is presently engaged with the quest for peace. I am not religious, I'm reluctant to even call myself spiritual, as with so many words we claim to know, some still defy definition. However, I do have a saying that I sometimes return to and happen to think it coexists with peace: My god is love, my religion is life, and I put my faith in truth.

Maybe I'll return to the Holy Land one day. I'll again trace Jesus' final footsteps down the Via Dolorosa, stopping at Abu Shukri's for a bowl of hummus and Arabic coffee. (Someone in history needs to be blessed for first deciding to grind cardamom pods and coffee beans together.) I'll then head to the Western Wall to see Muslims making their way to the Al-Aqsa Mosque on the Temple Mount to pray, Jews will fill the stone square below, lamenting and capturing their prayers on little white slips of paper and placing them between the cracks in the stone at the base of the wall, and Christians will pass by me on their way to the Church of the Holy Sepulchre. I won't see any soldiers with big black boots on their feet and guns held like a loved one in their arms. What place do soldiers and guns have in a city finally discovered to be holy?

Market traders will scent the morning with aromatic scents, spices and sweetness coating the air. The Holy Land will be shared. There will be no more fear and greed; hatred will have been allowed to be buried with the past. There will be only life and the love of it. I'll come to stand amongst this harmony, with the Middle Eastern sun watching over the ancient stone city. In this setting I will recall a passage by another Matthew, written 2,000 years before I ever considered putting thoughts to paper. I wish to conclude this book with his words, words Jesus is claimed to have delivered, and let them inspire us to do all we can to break the walls between us down: *"Blessed are the peacemakers, for they will be called the children of God."*

Afterword

April 2014 – Auschwitz concentration and extermination camp, Poland.

The tourists disembark from the minibus and blend into the crowd as they come to stand on the edge of the car park and before the entrance to Auschwitz I, the location of a permanent museum and memorial. No. This is not sufficient. We are standing at the entrance to a site on which one of the greatest human atrocities of the modern era took place; we are standing at the gates which open to the history of the Holocaust, gates which open to a history of hell.

"Okay!" shouts a large man with a bald crown and stress lines on his face to match the crease lines on his shirt. "We're going to split you into groups: French speakers to my right please. German speakers also to my right. Spanish can stay here in the middle. And English to my left. Thank you."

The tourists quickly splinter into the appropriate languages and as I move into the English-speaking group, I imagine the separation that took place here between 1940 and 1945. The prisoners that arrived at Auschwitz from across Europe: Poles, Gypsies, Jehovah's Witnesses, homosexuals and Jews, were brought for different reasons. They had either been caught standing against Hitler and the Third Reich or happened, by birth or orientation, to be a race or people who Hitler wanted removed from existence. The growth of Auschwitz from being a concentration camp in 1940, initially housing the overspill of Polish prisoners, to becoming one of the largest extermination camps in operation during the Second World War has become a terrifying symbol of what true evil can do. Today, green grass grows around the red brick buildings and the sunshine shimmers off the spring leaves on the trees, but the horror that befell this place has not been erased. It will never be forgotten.

With our English guide now speaking through our headphones the tourists enter the interior of Auschwitz I, positioning our sunglasses as we peer up at the iron words over the gate. We read the German phrase that inmates would have looked up at after first arriving at Auschwitz or as they left the camp each day to labour for the Third Reich, *Arbeit macht frei* (Work makes free). But not everyone arriving at Auschwitz was to be incarcerated in the camp.

As the war continued, Hitler intensified his commitment to the Final Solution – the eradication of the Jewish race. Extermination camps were established across Europe and Jews were murdered in their thousands, hundreds of thousands and, by the war's end, in their millions. Largely due to its location in central Europe, Auschwitz became one of the largest camps; it became a factory of death. The first building we walk towards is the gas chamber which operated in Auschwitz I. We enter and move through the windowless rooms. Each room has open hatches on the roof, allowing streams of daylight to enter. It was through these hatches that the Zyklon B pellets, a lethal concoction of cyanide and pesticide, were released into the chambers. The heat from the many victim's huddled inside was enough to release the gas from the pellets. Until this moment the Jewish victims crammed inside had probably not known they were going to be killed. On arrival to Auschwitz they were told they were going to be disinfected before joining the other prisoners in the concentration camp. They were instructed to undress and enter the chamber. Of course they would have been terrified. Most would have already been suffering from starvation and perpetual fear after having lived in the ghettos the Nazis had initially created in the cities they occupied. After a despairing journey to Auschwitz, they would have been led into the dark chambers where we now stood with smartphones capturing the scratches on the walls, and the sound of footsteps echoing around us as the line of tourists followed the route the naked and humiliated Jews would have walked.

We come to stand in the largest chamber;

the hatches are open above our heads. In this darkness the victims would have stood silently and looked into the wide eyes of the person standing beside them, perhaps mothers would have held their childrens' little hands as they waited, squishing them in reassurance that everything would be okay. The guards who had led them into the chamber would leave and a heavy door would slam behind them. There would then be a silence before the gas was released. The victims died a death preceded by panic and screaming as they suffocated. After twenty minutes, electric fans would remove the gas from the chamber, and prisoners who were given the charge of removing the bodies would enter. The tourists walk into the next room where two furnaces have been restored after being destroyed by the SS in an attempt to cover their crimes shortly before the camp was liberated by Soviet forces in 1945. The corpses would have been slid into the burning infernos and almost all trace of their existence incinerated to ash. The chamber door would again be opened and the next batch of victims would be led in, commanded to remove their clothes and be ready for disinfection.

Auschwitz I is one part of the Auschwitz complex which comprises of over forty camps and sub-camps. The number of Jews being sent to Auschwitz had dramatically increased with trains arriving carrying thousands, so the Nazis expanded the complex with Auschwitz II- Birkenau, located a couple of kilometres from Auschwitz I. This was the largest camp, with a capacity of 100,000 prisoners. It was on this site that the mass exterminations took place inside four gas chambers, dismantled by the Nazis in the winter of 1944. Our tour is destined for Birkenau, but first we continue to follow our guide around Auschwitz I.

Behind the crematorium is a building which comprised the SS headquarters. Here the organisation and running of the camp were managed. Not far away a beautiful garden grows around a house which was home to the first commander of Auschwitz, Rudolf Höss. It is hard to imagine that Höss lived in this house with his family, knowing that his children would run and play in a garden that was a stone's throw from a site where people were tortured and systematically murdered. Blossom is dislodged from the trees and falls around the gallows where Höss was hanged for his crimes against humanity in 1947, in the shadow of the crematorium's chimney.

"His wife was recorded as saying that they had been very happy living here," our guide tells us. "This way please," she adds, beckoning us to follow.

We walk away from the gallows and pass the blocks which had housed the camp inmates in squalid living conditions. Hundreds of prisoners would have been forced to live in these red brick prisons. In the early days of the camp's existence they would be forced to sleep on a thin layer of straw on a concrete floor before they were crammed into three-tier bunks. Our guide outlines the torment of living in Auschwitz, with many inmates perishing due to the conditions they were forced to exist in. In a given day they would only be allowed to use the communal toilets two times and for a very short period, with the weakest sometimes unable to push through the desperate crowd to relieve themselves. An inmate could be shot or tortured for trying to go to the toilet outside of this time. This simple bodily function could be the only reason an SS officer needed to kill you.

The inmates were sustained on a daily diet that would keep them alive but leave them malnourished and perpetually hungry; many starved to death or died in the factories and fields where they were forced to work more than twelve hours a day. Inmates were also subjected to roll call twice a day, normally lasting around two hours on average. In this time they would be forced to stand in lines in the scorching heat of summer or the freezing cold of winter, as the camp guards made sure no prisoners had escaped. An inmate could be shot if they shuffled or tried to relieve a cramp during this period of standing. Life in the concentration camp was a daily cycle of humiliation, abuse, torture, thirst, hunger, fear and inconceivable terror.

As we continue past the blocks some are mentioned for the functions they had served. We learn that one was the site of sterilisation trials conducted on Jewish women in an attempt to explore different means of mass extermination; another served as the camp's kitchen which provided the inmates who worked inside a slightly better condition as they would have more chance of acquiring food. Then we arrive at Block 11, "The Death Block."

This building was primarily used by the Nazi's to punish prisoners who had tried to escape or make contact with the outside world. In the first room of the building is a large wooden table where SS officers would decide the fate of an inmate. Sometimes the trials lasted no longer than one minute. The inmates would be subjected to confinement and starvation in dark cells, their sentence lasting up to several weeks in some cases. We trace the narrow hallways downstairs, peering through the peep holes and into the cells where prisoners were locked in rooms furnished only with darkness, silence and stench.

In the final chamber in the basement we are shown the standing cells. Sentenced inmates would have to enter through a low hatch on hands and knees and into a prison smaller than one square-metre. In this space up to four prisoners would be incarcerated with only a small opening allowing air into the cell. They would be subjected to standing for hours on end and most were starved to death. These extreme punishments were used by the Nazi's to make examples of the prisoners, designed to remove any thought of escape or sabotage from the other inmates' minds.

Upstairs and breathing deeply in the daylight pouring through the windows we look upon a room with a long wash basin inside. Prison uniforms are draped over it; black and white strips are sewn down the length of a pair of trousers, faded and ragged. The clothes belonged to inmates who had been sentenced to die by another means, and in this room they would have been forced to disrobe before their execution. In a courtyard beside Block 11 a grey wall has been reconstructed at one end, known as the "Death Wall". First, women would have been brought from Block 11 into the courtyard, commanded to stand naked and in pairs, facing the wall. An SS soldier would then walk towards them from behind and methodically shoot them in the back of the head. Once all of the women had been killed and their bodies removed by inmates, the men would suffer the same fate. Our group stands observing the wall in solemnity as the first crack of thunder reaches us from the distant sky. My head and shoulders suddenly feel heavy. Before visiting Auschwitz you try to ready yourself for what you might learn and see, but as each minute of the tour passes and the depths of horror deepen you feel the spirit inside you deflate. You begin to form a distressing picture of what took place here.

"This way, please," says the tour guide.

Swallowing a lump in my throat I turn with the group and look up at the wooden "post" where prisoners were hung on a hook by their wrists which had been tied behind their back. This SS punishment would often result in inmates falling unconscious from the excruciating pain or the tendons in their shoulders being ripped as the weight of their body pulled them down.

We leave the courtyard and walk slowly away. The next block we visit is used to display a permanent collection of items and possessions that had once belonged to the prisoners. Before deportation, people were instructed to pack only their most essential and treasured belongings, deceived that they would have need of them. The museum's collection includes some 110,000 shoes, over 3,000 suitcases, and rooms filled by prosthetic limbs, reading glasses and kitchen wares. A sight which will be forever imprinted on my mind is that of a long glass window spanning the length of a room, behind which is a mound of human hair, the colour of the different strands now faded with some still tied in plaits and ponytails. We're told the Nazis used the hair shaven from prisoners in factories to make fabric usually made from horse hair.

Outside we are led back past the camp kitchen and towards the main gate, coming to realise the great lie the inmates were told each day as they were marched out of the camp to the fields and factories, *Arbeit macht frei.*

Another crack of thunder sounds as the bottom of the horizon darkens.

"A storm's coming," I say to a fellow Englishman walking beside me.

He nods but says nothing as we return our headphones and leave the interior of Auschwitz I. The heavens grumble again and we are directed to our minibus and told we'll be departing for Auschwitz II-Birkenau in a few minutes. The tourists sit on the minibus and wait. We are silent.

The rusty steel tracks pass under the watchtower. Trains carrying thousands of distressed Jews would have trundled slowly forwards on this final stretch of railway. The gates open and the train enters into the heart of Birkenau. The storm clouds have followed us on the short journey from Auschwitz I and now sit heavy over the vast grounds of the concentration and death camp. Occasionally fierce bolts of lightning strike the trees behind Birkenau and swollen raindrops begin to fall on us as we are taken beneath the watchtower and guided towards a row of stable-like buildings. I try to stop the facts and figures I had scribbled onto my palm from running as the rain strengthens.

Walking through an opening in the electric fence which traces the parameters of the camp, we are told that when the numbers of prisoners began to rise, the Nazis brought in prefabricated stables to house them. The buildings were initially designed to stable fifty-two field horses. In Birkenau, however, they housed 400 prisoners in conditions so basic and unsanitary that it was no surprise to learn how TB, typhus and other infections were a constant threat to the inmates' already fragile lives.

We enter one of the wooden buildings, a large bunk house, with rows of three-tier wooden beds filling the inside. In these beds inmates would be forced to sleep together, sometimes ten to a bunk and often next to people suffering from diarrhoea caused by illness or starvation. Like Auschwitz I, inmates at Birkenau were restricted from using the toilets and many could not control themselves. The floors of the bunk houses would have been wet and muddy in winter, the mattresses of the beds would be stained with faeces and urine, and the stench in summer along with the stifling heat would have made sleeping almost impossible, had the inmates not been so exhausted from labour.

In each bunk house a chosen prisoner would be placed, known as a Capo; his or her role was to maintain order amongst the inmates, to spy on them, and to be subservient to the SS. Often receiving better living conditions, the Capo would seek to please the SS and as a result would turn against the inmates, or in rare cases offer a display of compassion. The SS used this means of setting victims against victims to further divide and weaken the broken prisoners. Over 100,000 prisoners would be subjected to this gruelling and still incomprehensible existence in the concentration camp, but this does not even touch upon the primary purpose of Birkenau – the mass extermination of Jews.

The train lines end in the middle of the camp. Jews from across Europe would have been forced out of the wagons in their thousands and immediately separated into men and women, told they would be reunited with their loved ones inside the camp. The lines of terrified Jews would then be inspected by an SS doctor, and in a matter of seconds he would send the unknowing Jew to his or her death in the gas chamber or to a life surrounded by death in the concentration camp.

Children, the elderly or anyone unable to work would be immediately sent to the gas chambers. These were located at the rear of the camp and, as in Auschwitz I, the Jews were told they were going to be given showers before entering the camp. The SS used this deception to stop the thousands of Jews from breaking into panic, and as a result the majority walked in silence to the chambers and their death. Inside they were forced to remove their clothes before they were ushered into the largest of chambers in which the Nazis had installed shower heads to maintain their lie. It was through these shower heads that the gas would be released. Prisoners from the camp would then be given the charge of retrieving the bodies from the chamber before they were incinerated. Survivors of Birkenau record how the plumes of black smoke rising from the chimneys could be seen and smelt all day and night. It was via this means of mass extermination that over 1,100,000 lives were ended at Auschwitz. Out of these deaths, 90 percent were Jews.

Listening to these figures we look towards the treeline at the rear of the camp where the ash of the victims was dumped in large pits; the thunder is now directly overhead and breaks in long sonorous waves. With the rain pattering on the gravel the guide promptly thanks us for listening and smiles a sad and knowing smile from under her umbrella. We follow her and the railway tracks back towards the watchtower and out of Birkenau.

Auschwitz II-Birkenau is not an easy setting to put into words because it demands a writer to go into the darkest recesses of the mind in finding the words needed to reconstruct such horror on the page. I have been unable to find words for much of what took place and therefore reflect only a part of the primary function and purpose of this camp which operated on the outskirts of Oświęcim, a small and nondescript city in south west Poland. The detailed and harrowing accounts of life inside the camps are best left to those who were confined in them and survived, people who need not imagine what incarceration in Auschwitz truly meant. *Hope is the Last to Die* by Halina Birenbaum, a Polish-born Jew sent to Auschwitz during the Second World War and now living in Israel, provides one such account.

Back on the minibus I continue to peer back towards the watchtower and observe the last bolts of lightning streaking in firing nerves across the sky. The spring sun pushes past the storm clouds and a soft blue sky clears over Birkenau. The engine starts and the tourists are driven away.

*

I visited Auschwitz on April 23rd 2014. I wanted to see this Holocaust site because I felt it was important in trying to understand a part of the reason why a concrete wall and barbed wire fence has today been constructed around a country in the Middle East. I am trying to understand the State of Israel. This afterword is my attempt to share a part of my understanding of the need for Israel to be a State of safety and reassurance for its people. After leaving Auschwitz and on the road back to Cracow, I sat watching the Polish countryside blend into a palette of greens and browns. During this journey I found myself thinking that the victims of such radical racism and extermination should not be the proponent for racism and oppression of another form. The remembrance of the victims of this dreadful history should be the proponent for peace and compassion. They should be the stars that now glimmer over us and bring light to the night sky, to help us to forever rid such darkness from our future and shared humanity. We are born of love and love can sustain us. Love and understanding can unite us again.

These final words were written on April 25th 2014, the day after Israel suspended peace talks with Palestine after once-rival factions, Hamas and Fatah, announced a unity deal in a move to strengthen Palestine and effectively bring the Palestinians of the Gaza Strip and the West Bank together again. Benjamin Netanyahu, the Israeli Prime Minster, responded by declaring that for as long as he remains in office, Israel will never negotiate peace with an entity backed by Hamas, a group which Israel, the US, the EU and others classify as a terrorist organisation. The wall between us, on this day, is set to remain. But I write with words and with hope that can carry into tomorrow…

Organisations

SanghaSeva

Organise "Meditation in Action" retreats in India, the UK and Israel-Palestine. Please take a look at the SanghaSeva website for more information about the Being Peace Retreat:

www.sanghaseva.org

The Freedom Theatre

"The Freedom Theatre is developing a vibrant and creative artistic community in the northern part of the West Bank. While emphasizing professionalism and innovation, the aim of the theatre is also to empower youth and women in the community and to explore the potential of arts as an important catalyst for social change."

www.thefreedomtheatre.org

Rabbis for Human Rights

"Rabbis for Human Rights is the only rabbinic voice of conscience in Israel, defending human rights of marginalized communities within Israel and the Palestinian Territories."

www.rhr.org.il/eng

Combatants for Peace

"The "Combatants for Peace" movement was started jointly by Palestinians and Israelis, who have taken an active part in the cycle of violence; Israelis as soldiers in the Israeli army (IDF) and Palestinians as part of the violent struggle for Palestinian freedom. After brandishing weapons for so many years, and having seen one another only through weapon sights, we have decided to put down our guns, and to fight for peace."

www.cfpeace.org

Breaking the Silence

"Breaking the Silence is an organization of veteran combatants who have served in the Israeli military since the start of the Second Intifada and have taken it upon themselves to expose the Israeli public to the reality of everyday life in the Occupied Territories. We endeavour to stimulate public debate about the price paid for a reality in which young soldiers face a civilian population on a daily basis, and are engaged in the control of that population's everyday life."

www.breakingthesilence.org.il

References

1) United Nations Relief Works Agency (UNRWA)
Dhisheh Camp profile published online, accessed November 2012:
http://www.unrwa.org/where-we-work/west-bank/camp-profiles?field=12

2) Reprinted from *Love in Action: Writings on Nonviolent Social Change* (1993) by Thich Nhat Hanh with permission of Parallax Press, Berkeley, California, www.parallax.org.

3) 'Offshore Zionism' by Gadi Algazi in the *New Left Review* 40, July-August 2006.

4) United Nations Relief Works Agency (UNRWA)
West Bank women take charge, improving livelihoods and decreasing unemployment *rates*, accessed March 2014:
http://www.unrwa.org/newsroom/features/west-bank-women-take-charge-improving-livelihoods-and-decreasing-unemployment

5) The World Bank
West Bank & Gaza County Brief, accessed March 2014:
http://go.worldbank.org/Q8OGMLXI40

6) *Peace Pilgrim: Her Life and Work in Her Own Words*
Available to read in full online at:
www.peacepilgrim.com

Acknowledgements

I wish to thank Lauren Parsons from Paperbooks for first believing in my notes from The Holy Land, and all at Paperbooks who helped in the creation of a book which, until not very long ago, was nothing more than an aspiring writer's dream.

Thank you to those I crossed paths with in both Israel and Palestine, you have all played a part in the writing of these reflections. I would like to acknowledge the work of SanghaSeva and Engaged Dharma for giving us an opportunity, through Being Peace, to work in communities far away from our own, and for the invaluable support and strength you bring to the people you engage with.

Again, I wish to dedicate this book to everyone who is working for peace, not just in Israel and Palestine, but wherever conflict is taking place, and where you are trying to dowse its flames with love. Thank you to all of the Israelis I encountered who are avidly seeking a fair resolution for their Palestinian neighbours – you are an inspiration to your society and every single one of us.